jazz in
the bittersweet
blues of life

Books by Wynton Marsalis

Marsalis on Music

Sweet Swing Blues on the Road

Books by Carl Vigeland

Great Good Fortune

In Concert

Stalking the Shark

jazz
in
the
bittersweet
blues
of
life

Wynton Marsalis
Carl Vigeland

 DA CAPO PRESS

Designed by Heather Hutchison
Set in 11-point Simoncini Garamond by Perseus Publishing
Services

Cataloging-in-Publication data is available from the Library of
Congress.

First Da Capo Press edition 2001
ISBN 0-306-81033-6

Published by Da Capo Press
A Member of the Perseus Books Group
http://www.dacapopress.com

Da Capo Press books are available at special discounts for bulk
purchases in the U.S. by corporations, institutions, and other or-
ganizations. For more information, please contact the Special
Markets Department at the Perseus Books Group, 11 Cambridge
Center, Cambridge, MA 02142, or call (617) 252-5298.

2 3 4 5 6 7 8 9—05 04 03 02 01

Phelicia

—*this country and its people*
our sorrows and history
the splendors we share
the mysterious, healing
binding force and beneficence
of music:

life.

contents

preface

"Make it sing," Wynton said as we were sitting in a Burger King outside Bowling Green, Kentucky. Before we ate, he said grace. Then, "Let's rap." Most of our discussion about this book took place in unlikely places; we even met once standing in the tiny lavatory of the crowded bus the band rode in. The very first time we talked was in a small club in Northampton, Massachusetts. More than a year passed before we met again, in the same place; and then the next day, in Boston, we talked as we sat on a piano bench in Wynton's hotel room. The next time was late at night, over cold chicken, in the kitchen of the Manhattan brownstone where he was living.

A road book that reflects its subject in energy and form, *Jazz in the Bittersweet Blues of Life* conveys what you see on the road, what you hear, what you feel. "I'm going to express more and record less," Kerouac said in a letter before beginning *On the Road*. This book does both, but without stories that begin, "I just lost my pianist," and then resolve neatly when his replacement is found. Making a distinction about different kinds of writing, Wynton called such stories "journalism." Whenever I started asking too many questions, instead of observing and, finally, participating, he would tell me I was speaking "like a magazine reporter." This was not a compliment.

When Wynton made the major transition in his music to *Majesty of the Blues*, Wynton's friend, the critic Stanley Crouch, said, "[it] became the event of experience itself, not a description of it." As clearly as possible, this book's many transitions, like chord changes, indicate changes in experience, in how experience is conveyed musically and, on the page, narratively. The narrative's logic is one of feeling, not geography or chronology, and it develops accretively, elliptically.

The book begins in and returns to the summer of 2000, like a refrain, but its central narrative documents the period dating from after trombonist Wycliffe Gordon joined the band (which already included Wess Anderson, Herlin Riley, Marcus Roberts, Reginald Veal, and Todd Williams, with Eric Reed joining when Roberts left) in 1989 until the end of 1994, when the Wynton Marsalis Septet formally disbanded, already succeeded by the Lincoln Center Jazz Orchestra. It was during this period that Wynton came into his maturity as a composer. What has followed in such glorious profusion—ballet scores, movie soundtracks, the Pulitzer Prize–winning oratorio *Blood on the Fields* and the millennial epic *All Rise*—evolved from earlier works, from *Majesty* and the three–CD *Soul Gestures in Southern Blue*, and two major compositions, *Citi Movement* and *In This House, On This Morning*, that figure in this text. Our primary goal was to convey a sense of this music's origins in Wynton and his band's contact with people and places on the road all over America—really, around the world—the source of its inspiration, and, then, the range and depth of its impact. Now that Wynton is leading the Lincoln Center Jazz Orchestra he rarely travels with his musicians the way he did during his time with the septet. But the symbiotic relationship of Wynton's music to his life on the road chronicled—and mirrored—by this book has not changed. Moreover, the music written for and performed by the septet is the foundation for the extended compositions Wynton has written since. As Wynton's life has grown more complicated and his art more sophisticated, the essential connection between his touring and his music has only deepened.

"The road," says Henry Louis Gates, Jr., "is the classic trope of the Western tradition." A popular misconception, one I shared before I went on the road with Wynton, is that the road is somewhere "out there." When I first flew to New Orleans to board a bus for San Antonio, I thought I was going *there*. Only after many miles, many cities, many people, did I begin to see that "there" isn't *there*. It's *here*.

Listen.

—CV

I

picnics and parades

It's a hot, early-summer afternoon, and we're traveling west across Iowa on Interstate 80, crossing the Plains in the thirty-five-foot-long Winnebago that Wynton rides in when the alternative is flying. With two drivers—a professional from Washington named Keith Anderson, who is on his first gig with Wynton, and veteran photographer Frank Stewart, who often does double duty on assignments like this—and me, we make a quartet. Today is Friday, June 9, 2000. Late tomorrow we will rendezvous with the Lincoln Center Jazz Orchestra at Snowmass, Colorado, for several days of rehearsals and the start of a western tour. We've been driving for nearly twenty-four hours without a break except to refuel since leaving New York late yesterday afternoon. In the rear bedroom he uses as a study, Wynton has been correcting the transcribed parts of several Louis Armstrong tunes for his musicians. Earlier he had been entertaining us with recitations from a well-thumbed paperback edition of Yeats, concluding each poem's reading with an animated analysis of its imagery. Last evening, as we made the long climb up into the Alleghenies, Wynton sat down next to Keith, put his feet up on the dashboard, and practiced scales on his horn before playing some blues as a yellow sun set into the dark mountains. Then, before commencing for Keith's benefit a rumination about the presumed romantic entanglements and imagined sexual accomplishments of his passengers, Wynton asked Keith if he played basketball.

"I could teach you to shoot and dribble, little man," Keith answered.

"Damn, Newman," replied Wynton, enormously pleased at this early evidence of Keith's temperament and spirit. "What are you saying to me?"

Wynton had been calling Keith "the new man" since we stopped yesterday at a sushi restaurant less than a mile from Lincoln Center in New York. Wynton developed a taste for sushi and a love for Japanese culture during many tours in Japan. *I must have been Japanese in another life.* The restaurant was closed but Wynton talked his way in while the rest of us waited skeptically in the Winnebago. "You know, five o'clock means five o'clock." A few minutes later he emerged, smiling, with the restaurant's Japanese waitress at his side. "Her name is Tomiko," Wynton said. Leaning toward us, he added, "Let's hurry up before they change their minds."

Keith had never eaten sushi, but was willing to try.

Wynton ordered seven or eight different selections, as well as a glass of sake for himself. Keith did okay until he tried some uncooked fluke. "Don't kill yourself trying to eat that, man," Wynton told him, suppressing a smile. He was trying to make Keith feel comfortable, while Keith struggled with the raw fish. He finally spit the fish into his napkin and shook his head. "Whoo-hooee! That's something you have to get used to," he admitted.

So is the challenge of driving cross-country the world's most well known jazzman, who just now in the Winnebago is asking Keith about his family. The questions are as much a part of Wynton's persona as his trumpet playing. Wherever he goes, whomever he's with, he asks questions. And he listens to the answers.

I've been on the road more than twenty years. Every day I have the opportunity to meet lots of different people. Try to make connections between them. I try to understand what they tell me. The hardest part of hearing jazz is understanding what the musician is saying to you. On the bandstand, when you play something someone can relate to, they break out with "uh-huh," or "yes!" or "Preach. Speak to me, tell it." Or they just laugh in recognition.

Keith says he has a son he rarely sees. His own father, he says, disappeared from his life when he was very young. Wynton responds with immediate empathy.

"That's hard," he said, "that's truly hard. Not seeing your son a whole year at a time. How did it happen?"

Slow to speak, Keith considers not only what is being said to him but the effect his own words may have on Wynton. A friend has gotten him this job, and he is clearly trying to square what he's been told about Wynton with the constantly surprising, energizing experience of actually being with him. Keeping his eye on the road and both hands on the wheel, Keith nods and says he hopes to see his son when we reach California, where the boy lives with his mother. Then he changes the subject as he continues to size up his new employer.

"So," he says, "do you ever, you know, play anything contemporary?"

The question throws Wynton off balance momentarily.

"Keith," he implores. "We play real jazz, man." Wynton emphasizes the word real; this is a subject we will come back to, he is indicating. Later, when Wynton returns to his bedroom for a nap, Keith asks me and Frank questions about the band's recordings. He's interested in a long, lyrical piece Wynton wrote for his septet, *In This House, On This Morning*. "In its overall form," I could say, "The piece incorporates the order and parts of a church service, but with its rhythmic energy and sonic variation it is certainly not a 'sacred' work. Borrowing from a wide range of jazz tradition, it celebrates the equally wide spectrum of human emotion and national landscape that nourished its fevered creation on the road." But I settle for, "It's a very beautiful piece. It's long, but if you have the time to really listen you'll want it to last even longer. You can hear different parts of the country in it. The mountains outside Santa Fe, for example, where Wynton wrote a section in $\frac{7}{4}$, seven beats to a measure."

We cross the Missouri River from Iowa into Nebraska with a recording of Wynton's lyric *Marciac Suite* playing on the Winnebago's sound system. Composed as a thank you to the people of Marciac, a small town in France's southwestern corner where the band has been performing every August for nearly a decade, the music bursts with the joyous spirit of those people and that town. But the band's sound on the recording strikes Wynton as a little diffuse. "You like that?" he asks with feigned shock. When he travels, Wynton is always listening to a wide variety of music. He also takes with him a compact digital tape player on which he listens to takes of recordings that have not yet been released and marks for his producer, either Steve Epstein at Sony or his brother Delfeayo in New Orleans, measure-by-measure commentaries on corrections that have to be made. But not today, not on a recording already released.

By this time late in the afternoon, we're all getting a little restless. Much bragging about respective basketball games has ended in, "Let's stop at the next court and see." Just in time, Keith spots an empty basketball court from the inter-state.

"Newman, let's get off this highway and see what's happening. We'll see if you can back up all that shit you talked," Wynton says. "Ou-eee, I'm going to tear your big ass like the bottom of a check," he exclaims. His own self-congratulatory laughter follows this threat.

"You call that little hop a jump? I thought you had game," Keith taunts. "You just a little man in a little man's body. I hope this doesn't hurt your flute playing."

Keith is in his early thirties. He has a thin black mustache the length of his mouth. At several inches more than six feet and about two hundred pounds, Keith towers over Wynton; with his broad shoulders, thick neck, and large thighs he has a fullback's build. From outside, he is no match for the trumpet player's one-handed jump shot, but inside, under the basket, he easily pushes Wynton out of the way for rebounds.

"Is that what you call defense? You better call Red Cross!" Wynton hollers jubilantly as he scores repeatedly from the perimeter of the poorly paved court. Instead of nets there are chains dangling from the hoops, and sometimes there's a noise like a swing when one of us drains a shot. Games are eleven points, and we play one-on-one. These pickup contests are a farce compared to the level of good college basketball, even decent high school ball, but they are taken seriously. Wynton hates to lose, and the results of a game are analyzed in detail afterwards, especially by the victor.

When I first came out on the road with Wynton I used to play regularly, until one day, after butchering several band members, they asked me to think about doing something else for exercise. "You might kill somebody, man," they said. Today, with less competition, he has relented and invited me to play. But after scoring triumphantly three times in my only game against Wynton, I leave the court and walk by myself to the other end of the park from where we've stopped. I'm not a basketball player, as he knows. Nor a trumpet player, for that matter, though I had played seriously from the age of nine until I was in college. We were in North Carolina, on a tour where I'd brought my old Selmer Bundy; Wynton's horn was broken and at a sound check in Charlotte, in an old downtown church that had been converted into a theater, he borrowed mine, sounding notes on it that had never been attempted, let alone made. I tried to play something when he gave it back, and he couldn't contain his affectionate scorn. On another occasion, before a gig at Kimberly's East in California, I sat in for Wynton during a rehearsal. The velocity of the music was too great for me to keep my place. Wess, sitting next to me, nearly fell off his chair laughing. Later, at dinner, he told Wynton, "Watch out for your gig, Skain. Someone might be taking your place on the bandstand."

Now, over the incessant roar of the trucks barreling along the highway, I can still hear Wynton's voice. High-pitched, animated, it sounds a little plaintive, like a child's on a school playground on a rainy afternoon when his ride home is late. "Damn, High Point," I hear him say. High Point is Frank's nickname. Mine is Swig, given me when we were in Washington for a week one December. Wynton's copyist at the time, the diminutive, profane Ronnie Carbo, had counseled me at length in the art of greeting someone (a light touch at the knuckles) and the minimum standards of good dress (get rid of the button-down shirts). Then he began good-naturedly taunting me about the number of women I must have slept with. Wynton had picked up the inquisition and gleefully announced his answer: Three. Ronnie agreed. "One in high school, one in college, and your wife!" To the number three was added the word piece. Three piece, as in suit. Wynton introduced me that night at Blues Alley as Three Piece, invited me to stand up and take a bow. Riding back to the hotel in a cab, three became tre, and piece became swig, because it sounded a little like the beginning of my last name. Over time, tre was dropped. That left Swig.

Up close to the concrete abutment bordering the side of the road, I can only see the tops of the trucks, whizzing past. I move back from the road into the field of weeds above the basketball court and up the small hill that parallels the road, and more of the trucks' bodies become visible, and cars, too, of course, until at the crest of the hill, fifty or so yards away from this small section of I-80, there are so many vehicles moving east and west I couldn't count them if I wanted to. And the sound is overwhelming. Wynton's trash talking is completely inaudible now.

A series of houses rims the sloping field at the top of the hill. The dirty tan house nearest the highway needs paint. The owner has spent his money on a satellite dish, which is mounted on the roof. At the far side of the fence, where a street ends, a middle-aged man in jeans and white T-shirt enters the field. He is walking two Scotch terriers. Near where we left the Winnebago by the basketball court, an older woman in a red top and a tan skirt walks her black miniature Schnauzer. Neither person pays attention to me or the basketball players, though I can easily imagine Wynton striking up a conversation with them.

I feel a little cut off in this Plains meadow, looking out at the sea of cars, remembering how I felt when I left my wife and my children, whom I kissed goodbye first in their sleep and then in my memory when I boarded a plane. My farewells to my family were not followed by an amnesia caused by the road. Rather, I learned, my feelings went into a kind of hibernation to emerge stronger and sharper upon my return.

At the start of another tour many years ago, in winter, before a gig at a new auditorium attended mostly by rich retired folks from up north, I ran into Frank Stewart in the lobby of our glitzy hotel near the beach in Naples, Florida. After checking in, he and I followed a boardwalk through the wind-swept dunes to the beach. Along the shore, a few couples were strolling. I took my shoes off and tested the Gulf water, which was warm. We talked about our kids. Frank, a photographer whose career had been nurtured during a long period when he worked for the painter Romare Bearden, understood the twin virtues of observation and circumspection. He had left his two daughters to go on this tour. He seemed protective of his feelings for them, as if it were a sign of weakness for him to be admitting how much he missed those girls. We didn't talk then about the circumstances that could precipitate such an emotion. We were on the road.

Frank and I had been introduced backstage in Carnegie Hall, in the small dressing room Wynton was sharing with several other musicians at a benefit he'd agreed to play in. The closely trimmed line of beard above his upper lip that formed the hint of a moustache was, I would learn, a part of Frank's style that went with the Stetson he often wore and the vests or jackets, their pockets filled with film. Frank's dark hair was neatly trimmed, too, and perfectly combed. He was a handsome motherfucker, but I didn't know to say that to him yet, nor did Frank know to call me, as Wynton later would, tongue in cheek, "Massah Veeglan."

Holding a camera around his neck, Frank extended his hand in a friendly but quizzical greeting: We each wondered why the other was there. Over the next few months, as we found ourselves regularly on the road together, I feared Frank might be usurping territory that was mine. Because we were the only non-performing members of the entourage, other than the regular driver for Wynton's septet, Harold Russell, and the usual complement of road manager and technician, both of whom also had specific duties at each gig—setting up the drums, checking the lights, and so on— Frank and I hung out. Many of the people we met on the road assumed we were working together, and I suppose, to-day, you could say we were. But I used to feel threatened by such assumptions. They robbed me, I thought, of my individuality. The proprietary feeling about myself and my work I brought with me when I went out on the road took me a foolishly long time to lose, culminating in the only time I ever yelled at Wynton.

"What's Frank *doing*?" I hollered.

"Taking photographs," Wynton replied. "What are *you* doing? Besides bullshitting, that is."

Direct, honest, open to what was around him, Frank showed me mostly by example how to get along on the road. He taught me how to watch without speaking, a skill I thought I already possessed. Wynton reinforced the lessons. Once, coming back from a gig outside New York, Wynton pointed out to me the ease with which Frank interacted with the other musicians in the band.

"The cats love Frank," Wynton said to me. "I want them to feel that way about you being on the road with us."

It seemed a perhaps unattainable ambition. But Wynton meant it not only as a reflection on me but as an indication of his sense of the way things should go when we were traveling. Uppermost in his considerations, though he never stated it this way, was the absence of animosity. More subtle than that was the ease of interaction necessary for a group of men to live comfortably on the road and perform music before live audiences.

I remember a cold, cloudy morning after a gig in Wilmington, Delaware, early in my travels with the band. The Radisson Inn, where we had stayed overnight, was pretty much all there was in a downtown of deserted stores with boarded-up windows and doors. Coming into the dining room I found Wynton by himself, reading the paper at a table, his food before him. I slipped into the seat across from his and opened my own paper and ordered breakfast. We didn't speak until after the waitress had left. Wynton's alto saxophonist Wess Anderson, whom everyone calls Warm Daddy because of his beautiful, sweet tone and gentle personality, was just wandering into the lobby as Wynton looked up at me, raised his eyebrows over his glasses, smiled sort of, shook his head, took another bite of his eggs, and then sighed before we returned to silence.

This feeling wasn't here when we came on the road. It's something we created and had to keep feeding, keep believing in. Us.

Or the ride from Wilmington to Washington, D.C., a quiet ride until Wess put on some blues and the inimitable Harold Russell at the wheel of the bus started cursing and laughing about something. There was a recording session in New York coming up after our week in Washington, and then a benefit concert, all before the holidays. Washington looked stark as we arrived, its tree-lined streets swept clean and all the stone monuments hard and imposing. But the feeling of arriving in the capital with Wynton and his band on Harold Russell's bus was warm and inclusive, like the sense in someone's home that you are welcome whoever you are.

"We're not out here to be bullshitting," Wynton often said. He was referring not only to the music but to the life. The worst thing a new member of the band—and that is how Frank and I were treated, from the very first day, as members of the band—the worst thing you could do was impose tension from your own life onto the life of the group. I had to learn this, but eventually, in the same way I had joined him for breakfast in Wilmington, I could enter a room where Wynton was changing his clothes before a gig and say nothing, not even hello, if my mood or an intuition about Wynton's indicated there was no reason to speak. And it was cool.

Cool. How many times did someone use that shopworn word? And yet, especially coming from Wynton, its very sound took on new meaning. It could be a compliment, a putdown, a noun, a verb, an adjective, an adverb. He could make it come out as an insult, an epithet. But usually, when he was talking with me on the road, it came out like a mantra.

"I want you to be cool about," or, "I wish you could be cool about," or, simply, in response to some concern or worry I had just expressed, "Be cool." Nor did Wynton leave it at that; he *was* cool, unflappable really. I never saw him completely lose his composure, no matter what the provocation. Not that he couldn't get angry. But those moments were rare, fleeting, and invariably humorous. Even when someone had crossed him, Wynton could usually box his feeling, square it, let it go—only to find it later, when he was performing or composing, to be transmuted into an emotion that would move an audience to its own laughter or tears.

The first time I saw him with an audience his group had just become a septet. The new man, trombonist Wycliffe Gordon, was still learning the tunes and spent much of the night simply standing to the side of the stage, holding his horn. The septet had played two sets on a June night at the Iron Horse, a nightclub in Northampton, Massachusetts. I'd gone to both, taking my eleven-year-old son to the first and my wife to the second. Wynton had gone out of his way to speak with both of them after the sets, beginning an extended relationship with my family, especially my children, all of whom he treated as tenderly as he treated his own sons. At the end of the show, I watched in the cramped basement dressing room as Wynton patiently posed for a snapshot with three young women and then walked upstairs, where a man was waiting to speak with him. We had a mutual friend, David Monette, who made Wynton's trumpets, but we didn't talk about trumpets or trumpet players during that first conversation; we almost never spoke about such subjects.

The second time I heard the band, in November of 1990, again at the Iron Horse, Wynton told me they were going the next day to Boston and then on to Maine. That was as much of the itinerary as he knew. He invited me to join them in Boston and I drove myself there. The band was waiting for Wynton at the Berklee College of Music, where it was performing at a benefit that evening. Wynton had been honored in nearby Cambridge, across the Charles River; there had been a program with kids, and the mayor had presented Wynton with the keys to the city. Then he'd returned to his hotel, the Park Plaza, before taking a limousine to Berklee for a soundcheck that was well under way by the time of his arrival. The men played on for just a few minutes and then Wynton sat down at Herlin Riley's drums and Wycliffe took Eric Reed's place at the piano while Wess Anderson continued playing his alto sax during a long chorus of blues.

"The blues are a form, just like the sonata is a form," Wynton said to me on the ride back to the Park Plaza. This was my first music lesson with him, as well as my first ride in a limo. The conversation did not stay focused for long on the blues. Matt Dillon, a childhood friend of Wynton's from New Orleans and now, for a time, the band's road manager, was riding with us, too. A short, fast-talking man with a quick smile, Matt began rhapsodizing about a woman he remembered from home, and this set Wynton's memory rapidly and colorfully in motion.

"Man," Wynton said to Matt, "you remember how they used to go out of their way to fix me up with black women when there weren't even any black women in the town?"

"You know we don't discriminate, bruh," Dillon contributed. "Creole. Caucasian. We love them all."

Wynton said, "Brothers get all kinds of women, just not in the movies."

Matt laughed, and the driver cocked an ear, but before the talk had a chance to go further we were at the hotel.

In his room upstairs, Wynton ignored the fruit basket and bottle of wine left on a table by the hotel's manager and looked for the phone. It was dark outside the window, but the Boston Common below was lit so brightly and festively it might already have been Christmas.

"Got to call my kids," Wynton mumbled, in what I later recognized was a rare instance of explaining his behavior to someone else.

While Wynton talked on the phone with his two young sons, who were with their mother in New York, I sat down at the piano that had been placed in the room for Wynton's visit. A notebook of music paper was filled with tiny, precise pencil notations. I looked in Wynton's direction and then held the music, as a way of asking if it was okay for me to peek. He nodded assent. Lush chords evoked a romantic but somber mood. It was hard to hear them in my head over Wynton's voice across the room.

The call ended and Wynton surprised me by joining me at the piano. This man I hardly knew, I was just beginning to discover, could make a few words or the simple playing of a scale an invitation to reflect on the passing of a friend or the possibilities of a romance. And even though he was supposed to be on stage in less than half an hour, he was completely focused on our conversation as he explained that this piece was about someone in a ship. I was sure, several years later, that he had been describing the beginning of his Pulitzer Prize–winning *Blood on the Fields*, when the two slaves sing to each other in the slave ship's hold, but he sharply contradicted me when I said so.

In Boston at the piano as he played a little of the piece, the music took me to a place I could not name but was certain I knew. I felt a shiver, then a pang: I was in the mountains, a quiet, windswept vista of green foliage and golden sky, holding my father's ashes.

Now, several years later, standing on a Nebraska hilltop watching Wynton and Keith shoot baskets, I recall the first time I went on the road with the band—starting in the city where Wynton had grown up, the city where jazz was born, New Orleans. The band was rehearsing King Oliver before leaving by tour bus for Texas. I took a cab from the airport and from my downtown hotel room I called Wynton, who was also staying in the hotel, even though his mother and father still lived in the city.

"I'm here," I announced, sitting on my bed, looking out the window as a streetcar passed below.

"When do you want to get started?" Wynton asked me. "My daddy and I are playing a gig tonight."

"I'm ready to go," I answered.

"Well," Wynton said. "Let's go then."

I went. Into the city at dusk, with clouds coming up from

the southeast and the sound of thunder, the streets lightening as the street lights came on, then a brief, hard rain with a brighter sky in the distance and then the sunset an orange ball falling in an overcast sky. To the nightclub where Wynton's father, Ellis, and he performed; to an endless rehearsal the next day, a long rainy afternoon in a classroom at Xavier University. And then a few days later across the verdant Texas plains to San Antonio, before backstepping to Houston where oil rigs sprouted from the ground like trees, and downtown, at night, the wind whipped scraps of paper along empty streets by tall, deserted glass buildings, and where returning to our hotel late at night I yearned to hear within those manmade canyons the echo of a horn.

By now I have heard that horn all across the United States, watched its finger buttons pushed down, felt the release of air in its valves as if they were the pumping chambers of a human heart and the sound emanating from the trumpet's bell the breeze blown to every corner of the country. Connecting an airline employee on a tarmac in Oakland with a native American chieftain at a Gathering of Nations in Santa Fe, a waitress in Wilmington, Delaware, with a man walking his dog in Omaha, Nebraska, that sound—that music—unites race, sex, and class, bridging past and present, allaying the anxiety of living without narcotic and affirming the glory of great cities and small towns, the smell of perfume in an elevator, the rustle of a skirt, the siren-like call of someone's midnight footsteps, the rhythmic beauty of a baby's breathing heard in the morning as the door opens and the shade rises.

One night the tour bus started out in Boulder, Colorado, where it was spring, then drove through Vail Pass, where it was still winter, and when we woke in the early morning in the Utah desert it was early summer. Whenever I traveled with the band and heard its music, I underwent an emotional metamorphosis as dramatic as that changing landscape and changing weather. I did not believe I had lost anything but, instead, had found—what? Hard, then, to say. Easier to feel: in the happy exhaustion checking into a hotel at dawn after fitful sleep in my bunk on the bus, in the enclosing familiarity of road routines (hotel, soundcheck, meal, gig, bus), in the rhapsodic sensations of sight and sound as we moved along the highway at night to the accompaniment of some Coltrane or Mingus or, as often, someone in the band practicing or just playing for the pleasure of it.

"Can I call you Skain?" I asked Wynton in California a few weeks after that first trip to Texas, on a tour that had started in Oregon and Washington state.

"Only if you speak Skainish," he replied.

A few days before we'd been to a winery outside Seattle, with a view of Mt. Rainier in the distance. There were so many people gathered on the lawn that the ushers had to form a kind of phalanx for the band to get through, like one of them was running for office. It was a sight, the men single file behind the semi-official guards, walking past couples on their blankets and old folks eating their picnics and kids yelling and running everywhere, until they reached an area backstage, a tent really, where one of the band began playing a tune with a Latin beat, and another clapped its rhythm, and whoever else was there joined in a kind of dance. The crowd was in a happy frenzy by the time the band came out onto the small stage. And just as they started to play an old friend of Wynton's named Leebo, who used to play funk gigs in high school with him in New Orleans and now worked in a hotel in Seattle, ran onto the stage and embraced him. It was late in the afternoon, fragrant in the field, the sun just beginning to set, and every-where you looked in that crowd there was another beautiful woman.

And I'd be lying if I told you that beautiful women don't make you play better. Or try to play better. But not just the women. The presenter, who has worried for weeks about to-day's weather. The sweet grandmother who fixed you some cookies and asked if you could play some Harry James. That's your woman, your presentation, your grandmama. The whole place was colorful and happy. We paraded out onto the band-stand. Parades and picnics, a stage, a summer's day, the cats. I loved them. I just loved them. You could take away all the glit-ter and just let us play. Hell, we're from New Orleans. We un-derstand picnics and parades. And sweet things. And the blues. And making love and the wangdang doodle dandy.

The world is a hard place. Is, was, and will always be. But armed with that knowledge, you can still find a million ways to make people feel good about what we're all out here doing together. Could just be saying good morning or thank you, or looking somebody in their eyes. I don't need what you hate. Give me what you love. And if that costs you too much, at least give me what you like.

I like the late-night sound of the train, clunking down the tracks, through the distant air the scream of its whistle chang-ing pitches as it passes from one somewhere to another who-knows-where. It makes me feel like a boy again. I like the tenderness of an uncertain kiss which innocently begins with a question mark but crescendos to an exclamation point. It reminds me of adolescence. I like the way warm milk and honey rolls down my tongue sweetly, heating everything from my throat to my knees like a well-intentioned blanket in the dead of winter. I can return to babyhood once again in my mother's arms. I like the romance of moonlit figures, flickering on the ceilings and walls of rooms in places as diverse as San Antonio, Seattle, and Boston—dancing shadows in syncopated rhythm which know the unending story of each room. Then. I am a man.

I love the road. It's not an effort to play for people. I don't feel like I have to go out there. I want to go, every night, want to swing—hard—with the men in the band, with people. Willful participation with style and in the groove—that's swing. And once you feel it, you've got to get you some more.

When you are on the road, playing in cities around the world, each performance reminds you of all the other times you have swung on bandstands or in audiences. It's just like when you move out of one house into another, you remember how the old house looked in the neighborhood, how it smelled, how your bed was next to Branford's for what seemed forever—seventeen years—and how a particular song you played or heard with regularity bounced through the rooms.

On the road, this kind of thing happens every day.

On the road, something incredible can take place at any moment, something that can reaffirm or realign your conception of who you are and want to be in the world.

Not that it's not a thorough and total pain in the ass sometimes, with the routine of everyday—the plane, the bus, hotel check-ins, telephone calls, interviews, arguments. You get tired and say to yourself, "Ooouuweeee, Lord have mercy."

But as you step out of the shower and attempt on yet another night to avoid burning your suit with yet another defective hotel iron, you feel the beginning of a change, a little like a change of weather or season, except this change is internal. It is the feeling of something impending, like your first spanking, or first day of school. Or kiss.

Then as you don your almost well-pressed suit you realize tonight is the only night you will play in front of this particular

*group of people. So, in a way, each concert is also like an initia-
tion or some other one-time ceremony. That is why the intensity of this feeling is the same in Lewisburg, West Virginia's
Carnegie Hall and New York City's Carnegie Hall.*

*You drive past the hall, see people coming in, see the hip
and the unhip, and the wannabe-made hipsters. See the couples in elegant dress, the old people and the young, the fine,
the refined, and the granulated. Band directors with their students. People named Gene, or Mary. Alphonse. Ralph. Even
Nathan. And you realize that you've been given the opportunity to bring happiness to people, provoke thought, evoke sor-
row, or convey something beautiful that adds to someone's life.*

This is what I love.

II

one

Basketball is a memory, dinner a longing. We've been telling Keith there ought to be a good place to eat in Lincoln, to our south, but he manages to miss the exit.

"Newman," Wynton bellows, "do you think maybe that was the place to get off back there?" But he isn't angry. We're ahead of schedule; at this rate, we'll arrive in Colorado too early to check into our hotel.

"What time's the ballgame?" Wynton asks.

Frank checks the listing in *USA Today* to see when the NBA playoffs are on.

"Newman," Wynton continues, "why don't we get off at one of these other exits, look for a place we can shower, and get some dinner."

Keith and Frank both like the idea; they're tired from all the driving. Keith takes an exit marked Grand Island, a remarkable name for a town located in the midst of the prairie, and soon we're on a strip leading into town that's lined with several motels. Keith pulls into the first one, a Howard Johnson's Express.

Frank asks what he should get for rooms; "Two doubles," Wynton says.

We eat at a local steakhouse, watching part of the game from the restaurant bar. Wynton pays scant attention to the basketball on TV; he seems more intent on observing the men and women at the bar, several of whom are wearing cowboy hats. None of us says much, and when Wynton asks Frank and Keith how they feel—should we spend the night at the HoJo's and leave early in the morning—assent is unanimous.

Amazingly, we get off the next day on time. Six A.M. Wynton suggests we look for a "real place" to have breakfast and after a short drive we're in a prairie town called Lexington, its streets laid out in a grid, the land so flat you can stand on the sidewalk of Main Street and, looking either way, see the prairie beyond the last buildings.

We walk into a small restaurant called Dot's Diner, with a sign on the door that says SMOKING ALLOWED. Inside are twenty or so people, most of them elderly, most of them sitting in small groups at tables. The folks by the door stare at us as we come in, and I can feel other eyes in the restaurant on me. When was the last time three black men and a white guy stopped here for a meal? Finally an elderly waitress comes over to the table we've taken and presents us with menus. Small, almost frail, she has white hair and her voice is barely louder than a whisper. "So," she says sweetly, focusing finally on Wynton, "you from out of town?"

another homecoming

Nothing worse than a pre-dawn bus ride through mountain air in bad weather, even with Harold Russell at the wheel. You'd be lying in a small bunk in the dark wondering if each turn or bump was going to be the last. The heat was always up too high. But if you turned it down, you froze. You were truly scared but too proud to admit it even to yourself. That's why I always slept in the last bottom bunk on the left. Right before the back lounge. No falling from high places on curves in the middle of the night, and always someone to hang with or something to do if one became insecure. In other words, floor level.

The gig was over four hours ago. It's a funny thing after you've played a gig. You never think about success or failure, except maybe that for us it's a success simply to be playing a gig of real jazz these days. We could probably be conforming instead to the conventions of our time: play loud, get a hairstyle and some temporarily popular social cause, put some fine-assed, half-naked people on the bandstand, be in the mix. Yass!

All in all, it's a bad idea to go judging yourself after a gig and getting all pumped up or depressed. Any of the cats will tell you it takes courage to play this music for people. You can't rely on the beat that everyone has grown up hearing. You can't provide what TV shows like "American Bandstand" and "Soul Train" led people to expect from musicians. You don't even have a singer. To put your suit on and play jazz music, knowing that many people in your audience have never experienced any jazz whatsoever, you have to believe beyond the fear of rejection. But that fear is part of creating. It is also a sign of respect for your audience. You want them to enjoy it, really enjoy it. Anyway, once you've played the gig you have to leave, go home to the hotel, and feel fortunate to have played. It's two A.M. There will be another gig tomorrow. That's the way it is on the road.

I've been out here for a long time. Seventeen when I left home for New York in 1979. Late night, Manhattan. Have mercy.

I was scared and country, but lucky. People looked out for me. Generous people like George Davis and his wife Diana. Had a big dog named Rosco, let me stay with them that first month, gave me counsel and love like I was their son. People like Wilmer Wise. Brother had been playing classical trumpet for many years, helped me get gigs so I could have some money, stuck up for me when old-school conductors said things like "This boy can't even speak English. And look at his attire. Don't call him back." I'm not going to talk about my cooking, going from my Mama, who was a virtuoso, to mine, which was damn near inedible. Being in New York that year at Juilliard was really like being on the road. Then I met Art Blakey, who gave me the opportunity to play in his band, the Jazz Messengers, and the real road began.

We were traveling it today.

A Lovesong for West Oakland

Three thousand miles from Delaware, it was a morning like that one in Wilmington. The sky was gray and a chilly wind blew in from Oakland Bay, making it cold outside the Campbell Housing Project, where it seemed like I was the only white person within two miles. But no one noticed me. The group of boys and girls inside the project's community hall was waiting noisily for the day's guest speaker. That was Wynton. Most of the kids lived there at the project, near the site of the elevated highway that collapsed in the 1989 earthquake. The highway had been replaced by a street-level road named after Dr. King, but nothing much had been done to the brick project buildings that formed dark courtyards where kids played ball and listened to music that summer morning.

Following the recent trip to New Orleans and Texas, and for Wynton an overnight trip to New York to accompany one of his children home to the boy's mother, this was Wynton's schedule for the past month just before the tour, my first extended voyage with the group, that had brought the band to California:

- Drive from Texas to Alabama
- Gigs in Mobile and Tuscaloosa; Memphis, Tennessee; Athens, Georgia; and Atlanta
- Fly to Los Angeles to play at Hollywood Bowl
- Fly to New York the next day
- Bus to Princeton, New Jersey
- Back to New York
- Bus to Philadelphia and Pittsburgh
- Back to New York for performance
- Gig at Oyster Bay, New York
- Gig without the band at Town Hall in New York

- Receive award in New York at a reception, play afterwards
- Gig at Avery Fisher Hall
- Bus to Massachusetts to play Great Woods
- Bus to Norwalk, Connecticut, to play Jackie Robinson Festival
- Back home
- Fly to Washington state, continue by bus to Vancouver and then Oregon

The range and pace of this frenetic schedule were typical of Wynton's career since he first went on the road with his own group in the early 1980s. For an artist on such an itinerary, a stop-by-stop summary of engagements, each of them different, could never begin to convey the variety and magnitude of his touring.

The reason we travel to large cities and small towns is music. The places we go are all different and yet, over time, interchangeable. Like going to an elementary school and talking to each class from the first to the eighth grade. You feel like you saw one kid grow up in three hours, like you saw yourself growing up again. You realize how quickly everything changes—how it stays the same. So if they are black or white, male or female, urban or suburban, in a perfect moment you see one kid from picking boogers to picking pimples. And you can talk to them because the music has taught you that living is all right. And that's all they really want to hear you say, no matter how pitiful their circumstance.

This music heals people because music is vibration and the proper vibration heals. Like tuning up a flat note. That one note slides up into tune, damn. Everybody sounds better. Music comes into your body, you know. I can't begin to imagine all the people Louis Armstrong's music heals. All the people

Bach's music has healed. Beethoven. Coltrane. Not made them feel good—healed.

It's your intent. How do you want to make someone feel when you play? What do you want to give them? What do you want to reveal, or want them to remember? When your sound is full of love and soul and progressive consciousness you bring people home. At home, everything is on the one. Home is what you know, not what you have been taught. You go home, you remember the first time of things. But home might not be where you grew up. It might be where you're going, because sometimes it takes a lifetime to figure out what you know.

I can remember once being in a class discussion about religion. Now I loved Jesus because all black folks loved Jesus— my mama, my great-aunt, grandma, everybody. But in this discussion the teacher said that according to Jesus, if you didn't believe in him, you were going to hell. And I said to myself, that can't be true. I was nine or ten years old. After that moment it became difficult for me to believe in certain religious activities. I thought it was hypocritical. It was not the semantics of the argument, it was the intent of the teaching that I objected to, the desire to strip other people of their right to be themselves, to denigrate what they believed out of fear and competition, not out of knowledge, and damn sure not out of love. I couldn't hear what the class was being taught. And that's how it is when kids are being bullshitted by adults who are supposed to be guiding them. They can just tell something, a feeling. They don't have the vocabulary or the will to express it, or to argue. They feel it and know it. So that's what I remember when I teach little kids. They know something too.

And playing music can be as difficult as speaking up when you're a child. You might feel certain things very strongly, but

*that doesn't mean you have the vocabulary or the will to pro-
ject them. Thinking and speaking are two totally different
skills. Hearing and playing are also two different skills.*

*When you're playing, you could be thinking of anything.
That thought might not be in what you play because no one
knows where his sound comes from. It's just your sound. You
can work on it and make your sound more like you. But a lot
of musicians would rather play scales and patterns and live in
the glow of somebody else's sound. To be heard, you have to
develop your own sound. You might as well, because who you
are will forever be in your voice. A friend calls on the telephone, I know who it is. They might tell me something I never
heard them say before, but I know it's them. And because it's
them I know how to respond. Play something that sounds like
you and somebody else will come behind you and play something back in their own voice. If it don't sound like you, they
might just be on the other line saying, "Who is it?" Then they
get disgusted and hang up.*

*That never happens with me and Wycliffe. We know who
we're talking to and we love it. We were loving it that day in
Oakland.*

When Wynton had asked his band who wanted to come
along today, only Wycliffe Gordon had volunteered. It was a
day when the band was already in the town it was playing
that night, and most of the men had decided to go to the
beach, but Wynton hated the beach, hated the feeling of
sand between his toes. And he wouldn't have known what to
do with a whole day off.

Then you have to take another day off to recuperate.

Anyway, he was invited to come to Oakland, and this wasn't
the kind of invitation he turned down. So early in the morning
we were on the road, coming around San Francisco Bay at the
San Jose end, heading east at first out of tony Los Gatos and

then north, along the eastern side of the bay, until we came to Oakland.

Soon, Wycliffe stood holding his trombone while Wynton began speaking to the Camp Fire Boys and Girls about jazz music and dialogue. But before he could do that, he needed to talk about talking. Patiently, he explained that it was a little like passing food around your table. You took some peas and you took some potatoes, but you didn't take everything, and you waited your turn as the different foods came your way. Wynton wore a white nylon running suit decorated with bright colors. He spoke in an even tone, the same way he would at a rehearsal with his band or among friends backstage.

"When you learn how to talk with people, to converse, you have a better time in the world," he told his young audience. But he was having a hard time.

They were all ages, these boys and girls, and they filled the room. Some of their parents had come, too. Most of them weren't really sure who Wynton was, but they'd heard of him, or someone they knew had heard of him. Or seen him on television. Wasn't he a movie star? No, Reggie Green, the guy in the wheelchair, he was the movie star. *Boyz 'N the Hood.* They all knew Reggie, who lived here, too.

"I need someone to come up here and dance," Wynton announced. Five volunteers in City Kids T-shirts immediately jumped forward.

"Okay, now, we're going to play what you dance," Wynton said. *They danced and we played, all kinds of crazy stuff.*

One little boy in the front wore sunglasses. When he stood up to dance he carefully removed the glasses and handed them to the boy next to him. *Then we began to play a second line, New Orleans parade music.*

As Wynton and Wycliffe played, they began to walk toward the back of the room, toward the outside light. The boys and girls followed them. Wynton played the melody and Wycliffe provided both a harmony and rhythm. The two men led the kids around the block, and people driving by stopped their cars to watch. Across the street, a person stuck his head out of a second-story window and shouted a greeting. A block away a group of men standing outside a store turned and stared at the impromptu procession, which made a circle around the building before returning inside.

Picnics and parades.

Wynton wanted to continue the class with a question-and-answer period, but at first the children wouldn't quiet down.

"You've got to show other people respect," Wynton reminded them. "That's a basic thing about living," he said. "How are you gonna talk to me if I'm talking?" Who was listening? He found out right away.

"Mr. Marsalis," a woman standing at the side of the room addressed him. "Is there such a thing as a love song?"

The poignancy of the question stunned Wynton. It was as if the woman were asking, "Is there such a thing as love?"

Since my first days on the road, I have been visiting schools like this one. Teachers struggling with inferior teaching tools and outdated books, always trying to drum up more parental support. Students all full of undisciplined energy, skeptical of your intentions but glad to have something different to do. They have the nastiest coffee you have ever tasted in these schools. But I love one particular feeling that permeates this type of institution: the feeling of people striving. That same handful of parents and teachers and volunteers sacrificing so much of themselves to create a nurturing environment for these kids. That is the road to me. That's why I'm not interested in sightseeing. I want to know what is inside of people that I meet, what can I learn from the way they speak, from their food, how they dance, lots of things. Sweet and ugly things. That way I can understand, say, the difference between the feeling of Arkansas and Alabama.

Or of Oakland and West Oakland.

To answer the woman's question, Wynton chose Gershwin's "Embraceable You." Wynton had played the famous song several times in the past week, and each night it had been different. Once, the introduction lasted about eight minutes and the rest of the song was over in about two. He recomposed the song each time he played it, finding a new emotion in it.

The melody is not the song.

The "Embraceable You" that he played in Oakland was short. Wynton pointed the bell of his trumpet at the woman who asked the question, and she seemed to nod her head in thanks when he finished. The children around her all paid attention.

"Mr. Marsalis," one of them asked. "Do you play professionally? Have you ever played in Florida?"

"When I first started traveling around the country, I used to look at license plates," Wynton thoughtfully replied. "And I would see Florida plates and wonder: When was I ever going to visit Florida? Yes, I've been there. I hope you get to go there, too. You look like you would have a good time in Florida."

A little girl asked, "Mr. Marsalis, why did you come here?" I said, "To let you know that you can make yourself into what you want to be. Don't let people tell you that you are something that you aren't, like stupid or any of the bad words that they use to describe you. No matter how many times it's repeated, on TV or even if it's your parents, don't believe it."

After the questions were over, someone brought a cup of coffee.

Looking at the clock now, Wynton realized he was going to be late for his next stop, the Acorn Community Center.

His host there, Darrell Hampton, had been a star athlete in college. At the Community Center—"the Acorn"—he became the recreational director. He started coaching a group of young girls who wanted to run track, setting high standards for them, including a stipulation that they be on the honor roll in school. By the time they were teenagers they had competed successfully on the national level.

Wynton could see a photograph of them as he entered Darrell Hampton's office, a short walk from where the man who arranged this visit, Charles Douglass, had parked the van after bringing Wycliffe and Wynton from the workshop at the Campbell Housing Project. It was hard to hear, even inside, over the din of the speakers by the basketball court, with the blare of an incessant beat and the word "fuck" repeated every few electronic beats.

A while back, Darrell said, the police had been chasing a suspected drug dealer in West Oakland. The man cut through the Acorn courtyard with the police right behind him in a police car. Darrell said the police drove that car so fast they nearly ran several people over. He told the police that, too. He told them they obviously had no respect for the lives of the people they were supposedly protecting. A few weeks later, Darrell Hampton was arrested and charged with misusing public funds, a charge that Darrell said could send him to jail.

Because Darrell knew Wynton was speaking to the Camp Fire Boys and Girls before he came to the Acorn, he'd ordered in some food: barbecued chicken and ribs from a restaurant down the street. And he'd ordered too much, adding sausage and potato salad. There was enough food to feed Wynton's entire band.

While Wynton ate his chicken, he watched pickup basketball in the courtyard. Darrell had promised him a game after the meal.

"Hey man, what you letting those kids play that music for?" Wynton nodded toward the courtyard as he spoke. "Did you check out any of that shit?"

Two boys acting as disc jockeys stood behind a table near the door. Their loudspeakers, which they had positioned at both ends of the table, faced the courtyard. In addition to the basketball players and older people walking through, there were many young children scurrying around. A teenage boy on a bicycle wove around some of the kids, almost hitting one of them.

Wycliffe and Wynton had come outside, where the noise from the loudspeakers was so great it was impossible to continue the conversation with Darrell.

"Man, it's one thing for me and you to cuss each other. But all this profanity and that one beat over and over and calling everybody nigger is just some more blaxploitation minstrelsy. I'm more nigger than you cause I'se mo ignant," Wynton said.

Criticizing rap invariably cast Wynton in the role of reactionary. What he said about rap wasn't popular with people who listened to it regularly.

Art is an expression of how the artist feels life. Everyone is some type of an artist, simply through the mere act of self-expression. The question is, how do you want to make me feel with your art, and what insights do you have that distinguish your ideas from everyone else's? When someone tells me, "Our art is violent and ignorant because we're talking about what we see," I have to question what they're looking at. Because life here in a housing project is three-dimensional. Sure, it's populated by people who are hungry and need education and jobs. But there are also many productive people right here raising their families and making ends meet with dignity. The cultural and social complexity of life here is far too complicated for any art to mirror. Sure, art can give organization and meaning to life, but the sounds coming from the loudspeakers in the Acorn courtyard don't do that. Nor, for that matter, are they an expression of street culture, whatever that is. Primarily, they are an expression of some people's willingness to degrade themselves on record, to make money pimping poor black folks' lives. Modern-day minstrelsy. Step right up! What's more historically American than that? Only the word nigger.

"Shake 'em up," read the words on the cap of a man holding a liquor bottle on the sidelines. His buddy wore a green and gold Oakland A's hat on his head. Neither of them recognized Wynton, nor did any of the basketball players. They could see that he didn't live in the Acorn; they would have known him if he did. He was just a guy who was joining them for basketball.

All through the game, a boy walked around the courtyard holding a dead pigeon in his hands. Wynton could see him as he was about to shoot. He would be setting up for a jumper and there the boy would be behind the basket; or Wynton would have his left hand raised high, calling for a pass, and as he looked across the court he'd see the boy again.

You stay out here long enough you see anything. But you can't jump to conclusions, like what does it mean or where is the world going, trying to make it be something else so you can name it and dismiss it, shit like that. It just is. Was. Maybe the next day he threw the pigeon away and started writing this semester's term paper. You don't know. But it was some weird-ass shit.

The driver Charles Douglass had left to run some errands while the basketball game was in progress. Charles had taken Wynton's trumpet with him, and he hadn't returned when the game ended. At first Wynton joked around while he waited for his ride, but as the hour got late he became annoyed.

"Damn, man. CP time, CP time," he said. "Where is Charles? Where is he at?"

"Traffic like a motherfucker," Charles reported when he finally showed up.

"Let's go," Wynton said. "You got my horn?"

"I got it, man. And I'm going to get you where we're supposed to be going."

Wynton fretted about being late. Charles didn't seem to be paying attention like he should. Charles kept looking in the rearview mirror to see his passengers, and he seemed to be concentrating mostly on his stories about City Kids and a record he had produced.

And what did Wynton think of Darrell?

"Darrell's cool. He's doing a lot for the kids, and that was some good food," Wynton said. "Wish he wouldn't play that rap shit, though."

Just when the traffic was heaviest, near the Oakland A's ballpark, it suddenly thinned out. Charles cut to the passing lane and picked up speed.

Wynton was silent, looking out the window. The adults at the Acorn had been so earnest, as if they thought through their efforts they were holding back a tide.

My mama is from the projects.

Wynton remembered yesterday's softball game; road manager Matt Dillon had bought bats and balls and we'd played at a field near the hotel in Los Gatos. Dillon pitched for one side and a girlfriend of one of the band members pitched for the other. Some children were playing in an adjacent field. Wynton went two for two and his team won by one run.

"Is there such a thing as a love song?" It's what sings through *you when you're making love.*

Sitting in the speeding van, Wynton wrote a few more bars of a new piece. Working quickly, trying chords in his head as he wrote, putting an imaginary pencil between his teeth when he needed his hands to play the imaginary piano on his lap, he knew what his part would sound like, knew what it would be to play it. The piece was big, getting bigger.

It's like coming home, meeting all these people each day.

Los Gatos Hospitality

The message light in Wynton's hotel room telephone was blinking when he returned from West Oakland, but he ignored it. Whenever he stayed in one place for several days, the messages accumulated in the dozens. Word that he was in town got out and people started calling; kids he'd met at a workshop, a friend he grew up with in New Orleans, young musicians, women. And, of course, the people who worked with him keep constantly in touch. Life on the road could be defined in part by the volume of telephone calls, faxes, and FedEx packages he received. In a given day he might talk a total of a dozen times with his manager, his record producer, his children. Someone needing money might call. A woman that he met at a concert a year ago would ask for tickets.

A new friend, Linda Oberman, lived and ran the Great Bear Coffee Company and Los Osos Café in Los Gatos. After they met, she gave Wynton photographs she took in the café, which she operated with her friend Sue Ann. In one of the photographs, Wynton's arm was on Sue Ann's shoulder.

"We've named two coffees," Linda said, "Blue Note and Jazz Majesty."

Linda and Sue Ann were living together with Sue's husband. They had opened their café after the 1989 earthquake. Pictures of other musicians decorated the brick walls of their place. Linda and Sue stopped working the whole time Wynton was there so they could sit with him. Linda was the more gregarious. A rather large woman with a nice smile and a warmth that was mirrored in the café, she told Wynton she'd been a singer many years ago.

"I sang with Count Basie in St. Louis," she said proudly.

There was something about the way she said it that I knew she was a jazz person. She wasn't bragging. She understood what Count Basie meant to this country. I didn't know what had happened in her life, what the specifics were, but you could tell being with her that whatever it was, she was coming to terms with it and wasn't going to make you suffer because of it.

Everyone has something that has happened to them. When my brother Branford and Kenny Kirkland left my band, I thought I'd never be the same, but I kept going, rebuilt the band, and we grew. Some people loved it when he split, because they imagined how painful it must have been for me to lose my own brother, the tenor saxophonist in my group, someone I'd played with since we were kids in high school, to a rock musician.

But I'm still here. And he's still out here too. I've traveled all over the world, playing the trumpet and meeting people, and he's traveled all over too. You see, it hurts, like the first time a group of kids called you a nigger, or bozo, or blackie, and you were trying to be their friend. It hurts, but the globe keeps right on spinning, taking you and them along for the same ride.

Linda and Sue Ann love music. And with the music playing, it gives their place a glow. You want to sit there and warm yourself in it.

Their food has that taste to it, too, and their coffees.

It's like the feeling I used to get going to my great-aunt Marguerite's house. She had the tiniest stove in the back room of an old shotgun house. They didn't even have running hot water. But lord help us for what came off of that stove. Nothing but the type of food that would make old Epicurus lose his mind. She was a little bitty woman, but put something big in that food. And that's what the musicians always talked about in New Orleans. When you put love in it, that's what it becomes. I can't repeat that enough. I know it's a cliché, but so is all of that ugliness that's repeated out here all the time. "Get as much as you can. Look out for number one. More is not enough." Don't nobody apologize for saying that.

Los Gatos is a prosperous town near Silicon Valley, in the foothills of the Santa Cruz Range, where the band was playing some gigs at a mountaintop winery. Each morning the sun burned off the early fog and you knew it was going to be a nice day in Los Gatos.

Wynton had discovered Linda and Sue Ann's coffee house the band's first morning in Los Gatos. He ordered a large orange juice, scrambled eggs, bacon, and pancakes. Usually when he was on the band's tour bus he just ate cereal for breakfast. Two or three bowls. He liked Froot Loops best, or Cocoa Krispies.

"I don't want my kids to be musicians," he said to Linda over his scrambled eggs. His sons were three thousand miles away in New York.

Linda nodded knowingly, as if she understood what it felt like to be this far from your home, talking to your kids each day on the phone, playing some music for them sometimes, a lullaby if one of them couldn't sleep or a funny song just to be funny.

Linda.

Wynton ignored his messages this evening and immediately took a shower. He disliked being rushed like this, though it was often the case. Usually before a gig he preferred to return to his room, make some calls, order room-service, and iron his clothes. This was his time, though he invariably ended up sharing it with a friend. Within hours of his arrival in a new city his belongings were strewn about the hotel room, but he was meticulous about doing his own ironing. Sometimes he might permit a friend to help him, but he always finished the job himself. "It's like form in music," he said to me after I'd volunteered to help press a jacket. "You have to have a conception of the way the coat should look."

As he ironed his clothes in Los Gatos tonight, he listened to a rough edit of a recording he had made with soprano Kathleen Battle. He'd first listened to it two days before, on the bus on the way to a gig in a nightclub on Cannery Row in Monterey. The music reminded him of the vibe he and Kathleen had been on in the studio, hitting it one take after another, each take at the same consistently high level of emotion and musicianship.

Cannery Row, once the setting for a protest novel by John Steinbeck, had become a gathering of glitzy boutiques and eateries. *The highway there cut through several fields where, the day we passed through, migrant workers were picking produce, next to the buses that brought them each day from their temporary homes to their employment. A factory stood near some of the fields, not far from a beautiful beach. Our drummer Herlin—Homey—and I talked about the relative difficulties of swinging.*

The phone rang. It was Matt Dillon, calling from the hotel lobby to remind Wynton it was time to leave for the gig.

The night air was cool outside the hotel where vans waited to take us to the venue. It was even cooler on top of the Saratoga mountain where Paul Masson had his first winery, since converted into the spectacular setting for a summerlong concert series, with the artists performing on the portico of a stone church that Masson's workers had moved up the mountain stone by stone and rebuilt in a hollow on the mountaintop.

The courtyard above the church where the van stopped was fragrant of jasmine. Men and women in jeans and fancy evening wear sipped wine while they waited for the musicians. They reminded Wynton of people second-lining in New Orleans, stopping at each bar a parade passed. Everywhere there were flowers. The musty storerooms smelled of old wine.

The band's dressing room was directly below the main storeroom, but the musicians spent very little time in it, since they had arrived too late for a warm-up. *I don't like to sit around before I play. Generally, I'm right on time to hit it. I'd pull my horn out and play anywhere, in a restaurant, a club, an airport, it doesn't matter to me. I'm always ready to pull my horn out. So is Cone. Wess too. I can't imagine going a day without playing, or two days. Two days would be unbearable.*

The sky this night on top of the mountain was a little foggy but clear enough so you could see the glitter and flicker of the Santa Clara Valley lights, spread out in a giant vista below. The view was breathtaking.

Beyond the people in front of the band the mountain dropped off, so that even though we were nestled in a little pocket, with the grotto set into the steep terrain, it seemed we were cut off from the rest of the world, the way you are in a plane. *But in a plane you are confined to a small space, an outside observer. Here, you're an intimate part of the bigness and wholeness of everything. You feel that there is still earth in the sky. Makes you wonder how far the sound of our music travels into the night air. Imagine it taking off, like a balloon, on a flight that can go anywhere and never stops going, going from mountaintop to mountaintop, on up the bay to San Francisco, or south to Los Angeles, or up into the air to the stars or to other planets.*

How high does sound travel before it can't be heard?

And who is out there listening?

Miles Davis once asked me what I thought music sounded like on Mars. I said I didn't think about that kind of dumb shit. He said, "Oh."

Though Wynton preferred a tour bus or his rented Winnebago because you're inside a place, not waiting on line in a terminal or rushing to get to a terminal, he used to fly a lot, until he thought he was going to die in a plane that lost several thousand feet of altitude in a matter of seconds. It happened when he was coming home to New York once, on a flight from New Orleans, the plane cruising along nicely, no problem, and suddenly, zap! It started falling. They had to make an emergency landing in Atlanta and change planes. Wynton thought about not getting on that next plane.

To me, the most amazing example of quick thinking in an emergency was a flight in Iowa I saw on television, when the plane lost its hydraulic lines, and the pilot had to bring the plane down into a cornfield by turning the engines on and off. This wasn't something he'd learned in flight school, not something he could look up in a manual. He had to apply his knowledge and skill to solve a problem that had never existed before. He had to create a controlled circumstance, in coordination with the other pilots and the people on the ground. And he had to do it very fast!

No one's life depends on it, of course, but that kind of improvisation takes place on our bandstand when we're really listening to one another. There may be no score to follow, no directions. But the music has a form, and we improvise within that form. To do so together, what each person plays must have some distinguishable logic, yet it can't sound stilted, clichéd, or prefigured. And it has to be together, and more together as each moment of music passes. You've got to be yourself and do it yourself. You can't hide behind what has been written down.

You have to jump into the chaos and make its unruly spirit submit to a collective will that unfolds moment to moment. There's no more difficult skill to develop in all of music.

Wynton began "Sleepy Time Down South," which made him think of Louis Armstrong, of New Orleans, but Veal played something that reminded him of the cats going to the beach while he and Wycliffe went to West Oakland. He thought of the big-eyed girl who drove the van up the mountain—almost drove the van *off* the mountain. He thought of the music. He saw a young boy rocking back and forth in his seat to the beat and thought of one of his brothers, Mboya, who is autistic and still lives at home with his parents. When the family was growing up, someone told Wynton's mother that the Virgin Mary might be able to help Mboya get better if she dressed him in white and blue clothes. For seven years, all Mboya wore was white and blue. *He was still autistic.*

I remember when we lived in a white house with red trim in Little Farms, Louisiana. We lived right next door to a barroom. The woman who worked in the bar was called Miss Mary. She had beautiful brown skin and eyes that were compassionate and wise, but stained brown also. She would always give me good spicy boiled shrimp and gather me up into that ample bosom, allowing me to enjoy the benefits of babyhood. We had a sweet shop on the corner that sold Red Hots and Mary Jane candies, jawbreakers and pickled pigs feet in a jar. Old folks sat on their porches and gossiped, and people talked with a heavy country accent. Me too. This was a time in the middle 1960s before Martin Luther King, Jr., was shot. Stuff was changing from the old way to a new way of the old way. On my horn I can play what it felt like to be a little boy in that house, or to visit my great-aunt's, or, later, to anticipate calling my first girlfriend when I was twelve and lacking all social graces. Just her voice on the phone after braving the disgust of her mother. Sweet.

From the stage, Wynton introduced Linda and Sue Ann during the gig. As he played, he remembered a morning phone call from a friend whose sister has AIDS. Wynton talked to his friend a long time. *What is happening seems harder on her than her sister.*

Behind the audience, Rob—David Robinson, Wynton's sound and lighting person—fussed constantly with the dials and buttons on his soundboard, which controlled the volume and mix coming from the speakers on either side of the stage. An immensely proud man, he was as impeccably dressed as "his boys," who were playing on that stage. And as focused and into the music. When the band launched into "Down Home with Homey," Rob began to move his hips and arms. "Come on, Herlin," he called. "Lay it on, Homey." A huge smile on his face, Rob twirled in place, clapped his hands to Homey's groove, then quickly turned his attention again to the soundboard.

Standing on the stage, holding his horn, Wynton picked and chose from his experience themes to riff upon. Each of those themes took a personal form: the struggle for a better life of the Camp Fire Boys and Girls in West Oakland; the aspirations of Erik Telford, a trumpet player he met at the club near Cannery Row, who was too young to enter the club so Wynton asked the manager to keep the lobby doors open; the dignity of D.J. Riley, a man Wynton's age who had Morquio's syndrome and could no longer walk, but he still came to every jazz gig he could, in fact he was here tonight, driven up the mountain by his friend Charles Douglass.

Another homecoming.

two

In Leadville, Colorado, where we've stopped for an early lunch, Keith asks someone on the street about the shortcut through Independence Pass to Aspen. It's a sunny Saturday morning, cool still up in the mountains, the bracing air a reminder both of the winter that only recently has definitively ended here and of the next that will begin to show itself in only three months.

"You're driving *that*?" the stranger responds incredulously to Keith, as she looks at the Winnebago. "Through Independence Pass?"

Keith holds his ground. He's not taking any shit, even from someone wearing only a loose-fitting sweatshirt and tight jeans. "I've just driven this thing all the way from New York in less than two days," his pose means to suggest. He folds his arms across his chest.

"Two hours," the woman says. "Two hours easy. And don't look down."

"Thank you, ma'am," says Keith. "And you have a nice one, too." He's shaking his head as we cross Main Street, with its old mining-town stone-and-brick storefronts, to a restaurant. "'Two hours,' she says. Our directions say it's only, what, forty miles."

Soon we're on the highway again, a two-lane, fairly straight road that for a while follows a riverbed lined with aspen and fir trees. Slowly at first, the road begins to climb. More turns appear. The road begins to narrow. The trees thin and then, suddenly, disappear below us. The road narrows and steepens severely.

Wynton lurches from his seat at the breakfast table, where we have been trying unsuccessfully to play chess on the plastic set we bought in Grand Island, Nebraska, and walks to the front of the Winnebago. He thrusts out an arm to a side wall to steady himself.

"Newman," Wynton says, peering out a window and down a sheer precipice of several thousand feet. "Let's stay as close as we can to the yellow line."

"There is no yellow line," Keith replies. He's slowed almost to a stop to negotiate the passage of a particularly narrow stretch of road where a car coming the other way looks like it is going to hit us. Finally, as the car nears us, Keith stops completely, puts on the emergency brake, and walks outside. There, in the chilly mountain air, he directs the car past the Winnebago's side, which it clears by about two inches.

"Damn," Wynton mutters. "Who told us to go this way?"

Up ahead we can see snow now. Several cars have pulled to the side of the road. The snow in the fields above the cars looks several feet deep. Beyond those fields, past the first horizon line to some distant white peaks, the snow depth must be so great it never melts.

some good swing

Wynton could see Miami from his seat in the aisle of the bus. It was about an hour away from the hotel where the band was staying in West Palm Beach. It was one of those hotels that even had a dress code. You weren't supposed to wear certain things in the lobby, like cutoffs and jeans with holes in them. Rob had suggested we stay at this hotel. *I like to stay in a variety of different places, from the most excellent to the downright tawdry.*

Rob loves things of quality. He likes fine Delamain cognac and Cuban cigars. He likes to be dressed down and pressed. Shoes spit-shined. He loves conversations of all sorts, from the bedroom to the barbershop to the boardroom. Once, we called Francis Ford Coppola and stopped by his house to talk to him. He was talking about world TV and other issues. We asked him a lot of questions about his concept of modernism. We had a good time, sitting up there, two, three hours. He told us to come back whenever we were in town. In Milan we went to see Versace and hang out with him. Me and Rob, rapping to him about Roman baths and Italian frescos. Giotto and Piero della Francesca. About the importance of knowing who you are in terms of your cultural heritage and where you are in terms of the changing world. Rob and I want to do something, we just do it. Eat in the homes of people we have just met, break out and talk to the finest women we see. We just don't care. But Rob wanted to make sure we knew about the quality of this hotel and behaved accordingly.

When the bus pulled into that place, a guy in a uniform with Bermuda shorts ran over to our driver's window, shaking his arms as he did so.

"You can't pull in here!" he hollered.

"Oh yes the fuck I can," answered Harold Russell. He's from Tennessee. Used to drive an eighteen-wheeler. The company he works for leases most of its buses to rock groups. We're the only jazz gig Harold has had.

The band arrived in Miami around four-thirty P.M. Harold was wearing one of his Colorado T-shirts. It was quite a trick driving that bus through the crowded Miami streets just as people were going home from work. Harold smoked one Marlboro after another and drank some more coffee as he looked for the turn to the street the theater was on.

The night before, everyone had played some basketball at a playground in West Palm Beach. We took taxis there while Harold slept after the drive from Tampa, and we played a long time. It was winter up north. But in Florida we played ball in the dark and it was so warm High Point went for drinks across a park of scrubby lawn to a main street with its fast food and gas stations. It was the kind of street where you read in the paper about someone losing it, breaking into the local McDonald's and shooting ten people. But there in Florida that night it was calm and peaceful. Wynton kept on playing ball until finally someone said we'd better see if those cabs would really come back for us like they said they would if someone called the number they left.

Someone did.

They did.

And it was a peaceful vibe riding back to the hotel where everyone was about to break the dress code in their basketball sweats. The pool was still open for those who wanted to swim. One of the restaurants, looking like someone's idea of the Rue de Rivoli brought across the ocean, remained open. Or you could order champagne in your room for $190 per bottle—not something one of us was likely to do. The temperature was in the seventies. A sound like crickets made it seem summer when you went out on the balcony in your room, the surf pounding off somewhere in the warm dark distance.

It was warmer in Miami. Standing by the bus near an alley on one side of the theater, Lolis looked hot in his T-shirt and shorts—Lolis, Brother Elie, whom Wynton still called Eric, his real first name, which he used when they went to high school together. They'd drifted apart after that. Lolis wanted to be a writer. After earning two advanced degrees and holding a reporting job in Atlanta, he had signed on temporarily as a road manager for Wynton. But he didn't like this part of the job, coming into a city and they'd forgotten something or the meal wasn't ready or the band was late. We should have left earlier for this Miami gig, he thought.

Lolis and Rob were frowning because they had to unload the bus, set up the stage, and organize a soundcheck, and then everyone had to go on his own to eat because there was no meal at the gig. Both looked at Wynton, each in his own way, for a signal. But Wynton had some music he needed the band to go over.

some good swing 53

"We've got to rehearse some of this ballet. Let's go, Rob. I don't want to be sitting around bullshitting."

Wynton could sense Rob's hot response but he kept quiet. When Rob started to get like that everyone just went about his business and you certainly did not make small talk or crack on him.

It doesn't matter where we are or what the circumstances, Rob always comes through. We all can depend on him. Rob. We call him Sugar. Sugar Rob. Because of his ability to communicate with the ladies.

The band rehearsed until six. Then Lolis gave each man twenty dollars for dinner and most of us walked to a downtown mall a few blocks away. Tired from the travel and the long soundcheck, Herlin Riley, normally the most easygoing companion any traveler could ask for, was annoyed because he wanted to sit down in a restaurant where you could order your food and it would be brought to you. Somebody's dinner took too long to cook and the musicians had to hurry back to the theater to change. They carried their clothes in a garment bag and ironed them at the theater. Each man put his tie in a special case so it wouldn't be ruined. Shoes were carried in shoe bags.

Once Wynton opened his garment bag and there was nothing in it. Someone had to rush back to the hotel to get him something to wear for the gig. But in Miami Wynton hadn't forgotten anything. *We were upstairs in these very tiny dressing rooms, smelling quite ripe, and there were no showers. It was hot. We were late. There was no meal at the gig.*

Another homecoming.

The theater was named after Maurice Gusman, a Miami businessman who donated a million dollars to restore it twenty years ago, when it was in danger of being torn down. Like a lot of big old theaters in big American cities, it was built in the 1920s for vaudeville and other entertainments. Then it was a movie house before it almost became a parking lot. Now it wasn't even officially called a theater. It was the Gusman Center for the Performing Arts.

Walking out onto stage there, you looked up and saw all these seats, a huge balcony, and you thought to yourself about all the shows that have played there before. All the thousands of people who had come to those shows. Except not many of them had come to hear Wynton. Usually wherever the band played it sold a lot of tickets, but for some reason not in Florida. Or not in Miami, Florida. *We play the same. Once, when the J. Master, pianist Marcus Roberts, was still with us, he taped a whole series of gigs to compare how we sounded in different halls and clubs. And when he listened to all those shows, the good ones and the bad, he said, "We sound more the same than different."*

In Miami Wynton played one of his tunes called "Uncle Pete," which he named after his mother's brother, an uncle who used to be a trumpet player, too. He died an alcoholic. Fell out of bed and hit his head and never got better.

We've been on the road a long time. A long-ass time. Tonight I'm tired. When you get tired you start planning ahead, thinking about what you're going to be doing, where you're going to be doing it. You lose your concentration. You have to let someone else do that thinking. The person thinking about that has to be the person whose job it is to think about that. Because if you are supposed to be playing and you start thinking about how many gigs you have to play this week, how long is this gig, when are you going home, and so on, you change your relationship to the concept of time you must have to be a jazz musician. This might seem self-indulgent, but when you are playing concerts every night is Saturday night. You have to give the people who come to hear your music the feeling of a weekend, not the feeling that you are punching the clock. You start thinking about how many this and how much that, and pretty soon you've lost your sense of the present.

It's like that when you're playing. You have a band. A form. Now you're playing with the cats in that form. It's a blues and you know there's going to be twelve bars. That's the form. But you don't say before you play, "This song is going to be three minutes long." You might do that on a recording, but not live. You don't know who in the band might get hot. Sometimes you catch yourself listening for what you want to hear, instead of what someone is playing. You start evaluating the music without having heard it. Instead of living through the music, you try to plan what you're going to experience. That's like having a plan for loving a woman. How do you know what she's going to do?

I don't even like to plan the order of the tunes, really. Sometimes one of the cats calls the tunes. Or I'll ask them on stage, "What should we play next?" But you get a feel for it. It's a conversation. You might be thinking ahead of time about what you'd like to play, but you can't plan what Wess is gong to do in response, or Veal, or Herlin, or Eric. Or even if someone in the audience shouts out in a way that takes all of us in a different direction. That's what makes jazz dangerous. All your life you've been taught to control time, and impose some form on events in order to manage time. You feel that time is your enemy. It is ticking away. Don't waste it. And please, be on time, Be On Time. Jazz teaches us to be in time, and that time is created by everything you interact with in a given moment. So instead of imposing yourself, you focus on including everyone else. You know what you are playing. But just by this slight adjustment in your feeling, you can hear much more clearly what you all are doing. You can better accept and enjoy what another cat is playing, because it takes you into the unknown and the unknowable. Into intimate contact with the feeling of another person as it is revealed. That's why we love musicians with distinctive personalities, like Wycliffe. We call him Pine Cone, or just Cone.

He learned to play by ear. Started in the seventh grade. First jazz he heard was Louis Armstrong's "Keyhole Blues."

Lived in this real small Georgia town until he was ten years old, the kind of town where you imagine dirt roads and barefoot kids. Used to work construction. Took up the trombone to emulate his brother Lucius, who went on to work at a nuclear power plant. His daddy was a pianist. Played in church. His whole family is musical. He plays tuba, trumpet, drums, bass, clarinet, piano, guitar, mouth harp, and the Japanese instrument called "shō."

The pride of that family, where and how they grew up, all of that is in Cone's music. But on the bandstand you have absolutely no idea of what he's going to do. Except you can be sure it will be done with the utmost creativity and boldness. Cone never waits for a cue from someone else before he tries something. If he wants to sing he sings. He wears his ties backwards if he wants to; he'll play an entire solo on his mouthpiece with no trombone at all. Or hambone a solo. Then he'll look at us like, "What y'all looking at?" We just laugh and shake our heads.

Cone. Just his presence is a creative experience.

"The name of this tune is 'Modern Vistas,'" Wynton told the Miami audience. "And it's a description of the first people who came out of the ground after the world was destroyed by nuclear holocaust. All the survivors were underground and afraid. After time had passed, one brave soul decided to go up and assess the damage. She looked out and there was devastation as far as the eye could see. But then, as she was about to go below with the tragic news, she saw and heard a little something. She squinted and listened way off into the horizon. Damn. It was a procession of people, dancing to this groove."

Live at the Vanguard

We were beginning to swing, there were some nights that we truly played. When that happened, the feeling that had been growing in me since Branford and Kenny left grew some more. We were becoming a jazz band on the road. Except for Herlin, who was older and used to play with Ahmad Jamal, they had all been students when I met them. They began playing with me because they shared a commitment to the music and to the way of life that created it.

In the early 1980s, Wynton fielded a quintet that included his brother Branford on sax and Kenny Kirkland on the piano. After Branford and Kenny left to play with Sting, the quintet became a quartet, with Marcus Roberts, the J. Master, on piano; Bob Hurst on bass; and Jeff "Tain" Watts on drums. Todd Williams and Reginald Veal on sax and bass, respectively, joined in 1987 and, with Hurst leaving, the group once again became a quintet. When drummer Herlin Riley took Watts's place in 1988, the entire sound and direction of the group changed. Wess Anderson joined on the alto saxophone later that summer, and a year later trombonist Wycliffe Gordon. Then the septet was complete.

We were playing a gig in Saint Louis. Branford was still in the band. This night a large number of high school kids came backstage. One of them was Todd Williams. He played Branford's tenor sax and right away we knew he had something in his sound and attitude that was very different from other kids

Jazz in the Bittersweet Blues of Life

his age. A few years later he went off to the Eastman School of Music in Rochester, New York. Every now and then he would call and let me hear how he was progressing. He was so serious. One day I called him and invited him to play with the group.

Wycliffe was a student at Florida A&M when I met him at a workshop for the jazz band. I begged Marcus Roberts, who was living in Tallahassee, to keep in touch with him and help him develop his playing. After a few years Wycliffe was added to the band.

Bassist Reginald Veal, Swing Doom, used to play with my father Ellis in New Orleans. My father taught him when he was in high school. Veal loves to play. Sometimes I would go home to New Orleans, and we'd shed with our homeboy Noel on drums until five or six in the morning. Veal possesses the type of integrity and love for perfection of intent that is extremely rare. Eventually he joined the band and gave us a consistent and dependable bottom. A true anchor. A spiritual and creative compass.

As the band got larger the music Wynton was writing also began assuming longer and more complicated forms. Before Wycliffe joined the band Wynton recorded *The Majesty of the Blues.* Then came three other blues albums that didn't get released until later as *Soul Gestures in Southern Blue*, a culmination point for the development of the band as an ensemble and a takeoff for the growth of Wynton as a composer. And it was around then, after Cone came, that Wynton wrote his first long piece for the septet, *Blue Interlude.* Forty minutes long and hard to play, it took the band a while to learn. They'd play different sections of it at gigs. And then they started playing the whole thing, which meant if the band was at a club the piece took up almost the whole set. Eventually, the band played it at the Village Vanguard in New York. The J. Master had left the band by then but he returned for that engagement, a weeklong gig, and by the end of the week the band was playing so well that Wynton called his producer at Sony, Steve Epstein. It was a Friday night, and Steve was in the mixing studio working on an opera that he'd just recorded, so Wynton tried senior engineer Tim Geelan, whose official title was technical director.

"Cheem. We got to record the cats at the Vanguard. They're killing."

So Tim got hold of a mobile recording unit in New Jersey. One of the people who worked for them was in Canada and they called him to come back to New York. And Kooster McAllister, who owned the mobile unit, said he'd come without a deposit or anything because he knew Wynton and knew he'd be good for it. Kooster just stopped the rest of his life and came. All afternoon on Sunday, the last night of the gig, he and Tim set up. They put their trailer in back and ran wires into the back door and pretty soon they had their operation so they could even watch inside the club on a closed-circuit television. And Tim got hold of Steve Epstein, who was still mixing, and Steve came, without any sleep. Or just a nap. He was mixing his opera until five A.M. on Sunday and then he came downtown to the Vanguard later that day. Wynton's father and his younger brother Jason, who plays the drums, were in the city to make a different recording, so they came to the gig, too, and Branford stopped by. Someone said Lionel Hampton would be there for the first set, which began about nine.

Wynton had played, and recorded, at the club before. He already had half a dozen live recordings at the Vanguard ready to be edited and released.

The Vanguard is so small you just squeeze into the office or kitchen before the first set and wait there, or in the hallway. Friends of Wynton's crowded the space. A friend named Amy had brought champagne and cookies. And Stanley Crouch was there. Wynton had known him since soon after coming to New York. He has written the liner notes for all of Wynton's records. He'll be discussing a Charlie Parker blues and in the same sentence say something about ancient Rome and then he'll add a quotation from James Joyce. And Stanley was a musician. When he first came to New York, from Los Angeles, he played the drums.

Crouch loves the music, the nightlife, the feeling of a club lifted through swing. Because he writes such scathing critiques of things and gets pure pleasure out of verbal and physical confrontation, it's easy to misunderstand him. He likes to talk. But he also likes to listen. He knows and cares about people. When one of the musicians gets sick out here, in the hospital, first one to visit him and call around to other cats so that they can show some support—Stanley Crouch. Almost every night he is out in the clubs, listening to people swing, getting a better feeling for what is happening now. In a crisis, he is the greatest of friends. A man of uncommon depth of feeling and enormity of heart. And beauty.

So Stanley was there at the Vanguard. And Amy pouring champagne, wearing a short dress that hardly covered the top of her thighs. The J. Master sat alone in a corner of the room, meditating. Todd Williams repaired a felt on one of the keys of his tenor sax. He played the soprano, too. And he had taught himself clarinet, which probably wasn't so surprising for someone who studied at Eastman and applied himself earnestly to whatever he did. You asked Todd about the clarinet and he just gave you this little self-deprecating laugh. "I don't know," he'd say. He started many answers that way. But of course he did know.

"Deacon, you got it fixed, bruh?"

Wynton had on a new polka-dot silk suit that he'd worn the week before at a festival in Connecticut, when he'd invited Lionel Hampton to come to the Vanguard. When Mr. Hampton walked into Wynton's dressing room in Connecticut, Herlin Riley was so thrilled he took out his camera. The great man had played too early for Wynton to hear him, because the streets around that festival site were very narrow and crowded and Wynton's bus had a difficult time getting in. It was just a day bus, a bus without bunks, the kind Wynton used on a runout from New York or short tours from New York when he'd only be gone a day or two.

He'd had to iron his suit when we got to the gig in Connecticut, upstairs in a room that looked out on the stage. A young sax player came in while Wynton was ironing and Wynton told him to get out his horn.

"Play on a tune, bruh," Wynton said. And he did.

"Okay. Now. Can you play the bass line for the same tune?" And he did, perfectly. Wynton was putting cream in his hair and combing it while he listened and spoke. *You got to use every minute.*

"You sound good, bruh. Keep concentrating on your swing." Someday, perhaps, he'd be invited to sit in.

The band played on an outdoor stage under a tent top in a field filled with people. *Some of the crowd sat under these nylon half tents, to shade the sun. You could see the colors of their Sunday finest festive clothing contrasting against the green in the grass and leaves. A beautiful day and an array of people. These gigs are fun socially but can be a drag musically, because people seem much more interested in their ham sandwiches, and if some fried chicken is available, forget about it.*

You have to have your priorities straight when you play a gig like this. Picnic first, music second. Except there was a woman in a short dashiki near the front, dancing, and some people clapping to the groove. A pile of pure pulchritudinous splendor in that field. Just magnificent.

And Tanya was there. We were in high school together. She was a sophomore when I was a senior. That huge two-year difference meant nothing now. I started teasing her about how she wouldn't talk to me because of my Afro and my country accent. She said it wasn't the Afro or the accent, but the approach. She's a lawyer. Tanya wasn't interested in any flirting. I kept messing with her about when she had braces and she commented on those plastic, too-wide glasses I wore. I told her she didn't think that type of bifocal was too large when it used to sit on Lolis's face, because she was Lolis's girfriend for a time. She gave me that look that says you're crossing the line now. Then she paid me the ultimate compliment. "Boy, you gonna be crazy your entire life."

Wynton was hot wearing the polka dot suit that day, and he was hot again at the Vanguard, because the end of the room where the band played was small and you just started sweating there as soon as you started playing. He could deal with that. But the lights that shone right into his eyes made him dizzy. Sometimes they made him so dizzy he'd have to sit down to play.

Wess Anderson's son Quad ran into the room with his mother Desi behind. He was looking for his daddy. And Wess's daddy was there, too. He was a musician. That's who Wess played with when he was growing up in Brooklyn.

Everyone loves Wess. He goes through life swinging. Keeps his CD player on day and night. Bird, Sonny Stitt, Monk, Lee Morgan, Basie. He stays in the pocket. Wess knows a million tunes and will play anywhere at any time. If you don't know the changes, he will put the alto sax down and jump on the piano. Sometimes he gets depressed about the sad state of contemporary musical affairs. Wess knows from very personal experience that the world is hard. But Warm Daddy moves through life as if it were a series of encounters with other people in which he has a chance to cheer them up. He gives long hugs, always remembers names, looks clean, speaks in an animated but smooth voice, and always puts all of himself in his deeply soulful, heartbreaking sound. He is the last one to leave the jam session at five in the morning and the first to do the elementary school workshop at eight. When I look across the bandstand and see him, I know everything is going to be all right.

At the Vanguard, Wynton played a few notes on his horn for Quad, and Quad gave Wynton a hug.

In the hallway Wynton's nephew Reese, Branford's son, ran by. There were many kids at this gig. *Where is Jason? When Jason is in the house, I get nervous because he hears and knows all of the music.* When Jason was in junior high school, Wynton's brother Delfeayo showed Jason the first trombone part from Mahler's Third Symphony. Jason immediately sang the part from memory.

If the band was supposed to go on at nine the musicians hadn't made it. And never would, because it was after nine-thirty.

"Wynton, my man, with that funny-looking trumpet," said an old man named Clarence in his straw hat. "I'm glad *you* gotta play it, not me." Then Clarence turned to Todd. "Hey, man, *Tough Young Tenors* is a winner, man." He was referring to a tenor sax album that Wynton's older friend, former van driver, and erstwhile road manager Billy Banks had produced, with Todd and some other saxophonists playing. *Yeah, that was an excellent record, and good for the scene.*

Rob poked his head in.

"They could double the size of this place and still sell out," he said. Rob had been helping Matt and the Vanguard manager take tickets, because the band worked here on a percentage and you had to count heads together. But Wynton was going to lose money on this gig. He didn't like to talk about money, but just the recording that night would cost him several thousand dollars. The money wasn't important to him. Hearing and documenting the band was.

Lionel Hampton was sitting in the very front row when the band finally came out. The men began with "Uptown Ruler" as a kind of warm-up for *Blue Interlude*. "Uptown Ruler" was a tune the band had recorded on Wynton's three–CD blues cycle, *Soul Gestures*. Later the band played "Stardust" and dedicated it to Mr. Hampton. The set went by quickly. Wynton never took a break in a set. When somebody else soloed he listened just as closely as when everyone was playing together. *Otherwise it would be like one of those conversations when someone says, "I really think the Senate race is going to be close this year," and someone replies, "Yeah. You know what a dozen ears of corn cost me last weekend?"*

Sometimes a cat will leave the stage to have a smoke or something. I never could understand that. Plus I want to hear Wess or Todd, whoever. There are times when you leave the bandstand in your mind and miss something that could have made your whole week better.

When Wess or Wynton played a ballad, conversations at the tables in the back came to a stop.

Some of the ensemble passages in *Blue Interlude* sounded rough in a way they shouldn't have. The band would play it better the next time. First there was a break while the management cleared the room and the next crowd came in. The band ate pizza in the manager's office. Or some of the cats did. Wynton never touched food while he was playing.

The second set started with *Blue Interlude* and it was better. Out in the trailer while the band played, Steve and Tim and Kooster kept track of this piece that they hadn't yet heard and that Steve would eventually mark, bar by bar, in his summaries of all the tapes from that night and the tapes from the studio sessions to come. The band was going into the studio the day after the next, for two days, to record this all over again. Tonight they would play it a third time, in a set that began after two A.M. with "Happy Birthday" for a friend of the band's from Minnesota, a man sitting in the first row, who'd been at every set every night all week. Rob bought him a drink.

At three-forty-five A.M. Wynton sat in a chair in the manager's office and spoke to the people who came in to see him. He would be spending the next day with his two sons. Now he was too tired to stand. He'd be standing long enough in the studio the next Tuesday and Wednesday.

Take 1

Past the framed citations for "Hall of Fame" recordings, including Bunny Berigan's 1937 recording of "I Can't Get Started," BMG Studio A was at the end of the fourth floor hallway in a corner building, midtown, West Side. The studio was a large room, big enough for the orchestras that had recorded there, with a small stage at one end. Curved wooden panels covered the ceiling and walls, except for the long window on one wall that separated the studio from the engineers' control room.

A little after eleven, musicians were still coming in.

"I'm tired!" said Wycliffe. "Slept like a motherfucker all day yesterday."

Wynton was sure he'd done just that. Sure he'd watched a movie in his room. Smoked one of his cigars. Maybe drunk too much cognac. Then worked out.

Coupe de Cone.

Todd, whose *Jubilee Suite* the band would be recording, too, sat at the studio piano playing the piano part for his piece for the benefit of the J. Master, who was sitting in on this session. J. had never performed the piece before and Todd had no recording of it to share with him. So later, when there was a break, Todd would teach the part to J. before the band recorded it.

Tim Geelen and Steve Epstein kept coming in and out of the studio, moving the chairs they'd set up and the platform for Cone and the other horns, except Wynton.

"We're going for a more natural sound," said Steve.

"Good," said Wynton.

Through the window Wynton glimpsed another familiar face: Dave Monette, the man who made his trumpets. They didn't have time to talk now and Dave knew that. They didn't even really nod. Wynton just looked his way long enough to catch his eye and smile. There would be more people all day long. It was always that way in the studio. People came and went while the band kept playing.

Wynton walked into the control room, and Dave took the first valve of his trumpet apart.

"Filthy!" he exclaimed. "This horn needs maintenance."

Chicago Interlude

Whenever there is a performance of a new piece, Dave Monette just seems to show up. I never call him and say, "You've got to be here." He just finds out on his own. We'll hang, too. He loves to hear the band and get inside of our feeling. He says he's come to get his ears cleaned out. Back when I lived in Brooklyn with Branford, Dave would stay with us when he was in town. Whenever he feels I'm having a hard time, he'll call just to see if everything is all right. Once we attended a Gathering of Nations, a native American powwow held in New Mexico. The powwow was for me a spiritual experience. All the dancing and general communal feeling without the slightest trace of hysteria, and the transforming energy of a diverse people coming together as one, gave me some good energy to write music. A theme came to me in the New Mexican desert. And I remembered it by singing the name "Dave Monette" to the melody. The music grew with the feeling of the desert and the mountains and the thin sweet air out there. I put that into In This House, On This Morning, *as a $\frac{7}{4}$ chant entitled "Initiation." But when I think of that section of the music I always hear it as Dave Monette.*

The trumpet was made of metal, so it changed temperature when you held it and breathed through it. Which meant even when you were doing everything else perfectly, if that were possible, the pitch was still going to go while you were playing. You didn't actually breathe into the trumpet to make it begin to work. You made a kind of buzz with your lips, by putting them close enough together to cause them to vibrate when you blew through them. To do this within the full dynamic and tonal range of the trumpet required lips that were both supple and strong. You had to build up your strength by playing for many years.

Though it's a powerful instrument, you can never force the trumpet. You got to baby it, treat it gently, coax it. It's always there for you when you need a high note or something very loud. It likes to do that. If you don't handle up on it, it won't respect you.

Since I really began shedding on my horn I've always played it every day, even if it's just one note. I always tell young people who are just starting out, even if you don't have the desire to practice a long time, be sure to practice at least a little every day. Work on the things you really have difficulty executing, instead of playing what you know.

When you were first playing trumpet it made you tired, physically and mentally. Your lips were what got the most tired, and you could practice or play too much for your lips, so they got worn out, even after you were older and they'd built up lots of endurance. Even Louis Armstrong did this hitting all those high Cs early in his career, and he had to lay off for a time before he got his lip back. Wynton didn't play that high that often, at least not compared to a player like Jon Faddis, or Maynard Ferguson when he was younger. And Maynard could still screech out those notes up there in the stratosphere. For Wynton, the strain if it was physical was more apt to come from playing a long time. But that was relative. Many days he'd spent recording and then gone out somewhere to play late at night and then come back into the studio the next day and he was fine. How you played was more of a factor than how long. One of Wynton's old teachers, Bill Fielder, said it was all breathing. If you were not breathing relaxed, you were going to miss the note. If you were relaxed, your tone would stay steady.

When Wynton was performing, he tried to remember this walking on stage or walking around on the stage during a set. He never rushed out onto the stage. He walked slowly, with his shoulders relaxed. All the men in the band did that to some extent, too. They wouldn't want to play with someone who came out juiced. It would throw their vibe off, and not just on the bandstand. *Relaxing and being cool is a part of swinging and communicating. It's like dapping somebody. You don't want to put on a production, you just want to show them some affection. Dap can be just a nod or a glance. It doesn't have to be a high five or crackling snap with a bunch of hooting and hollering. A bunch of excitement and overdone gesticulations generally connote a lack of substance and of understanding for the nuances of a given situation, especially where some soul is concerned. Intensity without volume, that's the goal on the bandstand. And off.*

Homey, Cone, and Veal were all big strong men. And the Deacon was as tall as Warm Daddy was round (before he went on a weight-loss program and started working out). Homey and Cone were so strong they could throw a football fifty yards, and that ball popped into your hands or your stomach when you caught it. Pine Cone could bench press a few hundred pounds. He and Veal—Swing Doom—worked out wherever the band was staying. They were like athletes in their build. But when you met Homey, embraced him after a gig, he was gentle. He gave you a hand to snap, he smiled and his eyes brightened because he was glad to see you, and you knew you were in the presence of a powerful man, but it was not power that came from brute strength, strong as Homey happened to be. It was the same inner power that he had on the bandstand, the same certainty and confidence, and it was so strong when he laid down the groove there was never a time when the rest of the band didn't feel that confidence themselves. They might have disagreed with Homey about things, they might have thought their solo should have been longer, or he might have wondered when was he ever going to solo, but they always knew Homey would hold that groove.

"It takes a lot of discipline," he said. "I could really over-power everyone."

Another thing about trumpet playing, trumpetising, trumpetering. Another thing: You have to give yourself permission to mess up. You start second-guessing yourself, you might as well stop playing. The trumpet can tell when you're afraid of it. That's why it's best to approach your horn with seriousness whenever it comes out of the case. Then, when the nervousness of playing for people who have paid for a ticket hits you, you can handle it. You don't fall apart because all you know how to do when your trumpet comes out is be serious. You realize people want you to sound good, you embrace the experience of playing for them. Have you ever paid for a ticket for something that you wanted to be sad? Composing is totally different. It's about mental isolation. By the time you share a piece with an audience, all of your work has been long done. But you're still nervous about whether people will like it. It's important for you to want people to enjoy what you do.

When you play the trumpet just a slight change in the pressure of the air you are pushing through the tubing can cause a mistake. Some people who could really play stumbled a few times because of this and suddenly they couldn't get it out of their heads and they actually had to quit playing. I once knew a trumpet player who used to be in an orchestra who started thinking about how easy it was to miss and he had a nervous breakdown.

Of course there were other factors, too, such as overplaying, which was like overacting. You could overplay Bach. You could overplay King Oliver. *And you can encounter all kinds of difficulties even when you're playing your best. It's hard to hear inside the form if you're playing a tune and the rhythm section is not in balance. Very seldom on the bandstand can I really hear what Veal is playing, what the actual notes are. And rhythms are even harder to hear, maybe because of the way you have to hold the trumpet. It points out, not down. In fact people are always saying, "Skain, point that bell out," because I'll be letting it slip, it's easier to hear the rhythm. When I'm really firing, all I'm really hearing is just sound.*

That's also why it's so hard to be truly swinging. Swing is all a question of how long you can maintain an equilibrium with other musicians. Anyone can do it for one measure. But two or three minutes, or ten, that's a different story. You have to adjust to what everyone else plays whether you like it or not. Don't judge it or fight it. Work with it. Because the music is not gonna stop for you to get your head right. Plus, you have to feel the swing coming up from the floor into your body. How you stand is very important. Some stances are just conducive to swinging. If I stand up straight for too long it's harder to swing.

Plus my feet hurt.

After you'd learned the requisites of playing, the scales, fingering, tonguing, intervals, you wanted the horn to be there when you needed it, you wanted the notes to be there. You didn't want to strain. This was especially important in the high register, where it was so easy to go for one note and hit another, because the spacings for the intervals were so close up there.

You didn't want to be thinking about your horn at all when you were playing music. The two were so intimately related but so different. Monette, who spent so much time with trumpets and trumpeters, would never want to talk about trumpets when you were with him. You could ask Dave about the valves or the thickness of the metal, and the most he might say was, "How does that mouthpiece feel?" You could get him talking about mouthpieces. But otherwise he wanted to talk about other things, people, places. He wanted to talk about music. If you called and talked to him, and you asked him how he was, "Still breathin'," would be his usual answer.

Wynton mentioned one day that he was coming to Chicago. That afternoon, Dave was at the airport to meet him.

Several months went by, and the two men hadn't spoken. Wynton was even in Chicago again with the band and couldn't call because he had no time. It was a private gig, which he played now and then. *That's right. Once a while back with my Daddy and J. in San Diego, we even played an ear surgeons' convention. Mobbed. Biggest banquet room I'd seen outside Las Vegas and every table was full. By the time we finished playing half those tables were empty. That happens. People were tired. Those doctors had to get up early the next morning for convention conferences. And I was leaving that night with hoo-hob Sugar Rob for L.A., to talk to some movie directors about writing movie scores. We were going to drive up, meet my manager, Ed Arrendell, then catch up with the cats on the bus in Fresno. But I met someone nice in San Diego, someone I knew I'd call, and my Daddy seemed glad to see us. I worked on some of the piece I was writing, and you never know, the sunlight off the ocean that afternoon, how it made the water seem suspended out the bus window, that beautiful blue, the intimacy of the evening, you never know when you might be working up on a memory. The Navy ships in the harbor, or men up on about the twentieth floor of this building under construction next to the hotel, working long after dark, using a floodlight to see, and they must have forgotten to tell the police because a crowd formed and the police came by in a patrol boat and shined a light up on that building, you might remember that and put it in some music. Or the sailors for the America's Cup that we met in the lobby.*

You never know.

Damn, you truly never know.

Once, in Germany, on a classical tour, I had a long night-time drive on the autobahn from Marktoberdorf to Munich. I put a cassette of solo Monk in the car stereo. No matter how hard I tried, the driver refused to engage in a conversation. All the while we're cruising down the highway in the deepest part of night with Monk tinkling away. The cassette kept turning over and over. I created a character profile of this man. He was probably a Nazi or some type of racist. Monk still playing. "Just a Gigolo." "Memories of You." Bittersweet. I was in such a hurry to get out of his car when we got to the hotel that I forgot my cassette. As I was checking in, the driver brought it back to me and spoke for the first and only time. He placed the tape in my hand and said "Monk."

Nor did Wynton call Dave the next time the band played in Chicago. But Dave was already there when the band arrived at the Ravinia Festival. He was a kind of fixture backstage because so many of his clients played there. Ravinia is outside Chicago and the band was staying in one of the suburbs, going into the city the next day for a benefit at the Historical Society.

The night the band played Ravinia so did Gunther Schuller and his Smithsonian band. Wynton played some Louis Armstrong solos with Gunther's group. By his own admission, he played poorly. He never felt in sync with the group. When he was done he wanted to put it behind him quickly. *Worst I've played in as long as I can remember. I played so bad I was embarrassed to see anyone. When I got offstage all I wanted to do was leave. So I grabbed my trumpet case and split.*

"Let's go," Wynton said.

The next night in Chicago, we stayed in an old hotel in the Gold Coast area of the city. It was just a few blocks from

Lake Michigan, where Budweiser was sponsoring a stop on its pro volleyball tour that weekend. It was early-summer hot, a haze over the city as we drove in that afternoon, taking a short cut because there was a parade somewhere and of course the short cut took about an extra hour.

Whenever we come to Chicago, I think about how many people from Mississippi moved here. How did they handle this cold? I think of Joe Siegel's Jazz Showcase and the great Studs Turkel. Chicago is a bustling, hard city with a big heart, but it's cold too. As if that heart doesn't pump enough blood to keep the extremities warm. There's more segregation here than anywhere. I wonder how the New Orleans musicians who came here dealt with this big frozen braggadocios I-don't-give-a-damn of a place. But Chicago is sexy too. Yes lord.

At the Chicago Historical Society gig, two groups went on before the band, and there was a reception, too. So the audience was tired. *It was a hip crowd but the people were tired.* So were Wynton's chops. Monette fussed a little with Wynton's horn. He told Wynton he should clean it more often.

Dave wanted to hang afterwards but Wynton was meeting someone else, so they embraced outside and Dave turned and was gone. He lived nearby, but his shop was on the other side of the Chicago River. Wynton never got to it on that visit. In fact, he never got there again, because Dave moved to Portland soon after that. All those gigs, all those records, all played on horns made in that shop and now it was probably an accountant's office or a law firm. *The coming and going that makes life free has a melancholy.* The downtown streets darkening late in the day because the buildings cut off the light, the quiet flow of the river through downtown, all the people pushing toward the train station or the Loop, the stores, and Gaylord's where Dave had taken him to eat, an Indian place that Dave went to so often they knew when he walked in the door what to cook for him.

Then the band left the Historical Society, with its exhibitions of covered wagons that crossed the prairie that starts right outside Chicago, just to the west, and the men returned to the hotel, all except High Point and me and Lolis, who went with a Chicago friend of High Point's to get barbecue on the South Side. It was after three A.M. when we got back, but Herlin and his wife Pat, who was with the band that part of the tour, were up watching a movie. They called the other men who had ordered some barbecue.

When Swing Doom came into the room he wanted to know where was his that he paid for in advance and why was everyone already eating? He took what someone gave him, that he had paid for in advance, he said again, and took it to his room, too angry to speak. When Veal was on a vibe like that everyone gave him space. *Reginald, whose powders and talcs might have led you to believe falsely he was effete, also had a wild side. He was the gritmaster of the band. As such, he could hold a stare until your eyes began to water.*

Reginald deliberated over each thing he did, except for the crazy things he sometimes shouted in an elevator or dressing room, or on the bus. He might be in the tiny bus toilet and hear someone knocking on the door and he'd holler, "Ouch!" really loud, or maybe, "Who is that Mickey Fickey?" in a booming voice, loud enough to scare someone into shouting in response. Everyone laughed in mock surprise whenever he did this, because Reginald was a very gentle person, given to saying sweet things to other people, complimenting them kindly on their clothes or their smile. *He is an original. Unique, self-made, and unapologetic.*

Back At The Studio

Wynton was fighting a summer cold. He'd play through it, even though it could make hearing himself difficult. He always played if he was sick. *Nothing else you can do.*

Around noon one of producer Steve Epstein's assistants, recording engineer Mark Wilder, was still fussing with the placement of mikes. Steve sat in the control room in front of a huge panel of switches and dials onto which someone had written LORD OF THE SOUNDROOM.

The band still hadn't recorded a note when Wynton's brother Jason came in.

"I need some bread," he said.

The men in the studio were getting restless. Cone sat down at Homey's drums and began playing a blues. Wess picked up on the piano, while Wynton checked something he wrote the night before for another tune they were going to record. Finally J. showed up, his brother Eugene leading him into the studio since he cannot see, and they started right in playing. They started on Cone's tune, "And the Band Played On."

"Let's really work on this to get the sound, so we're not here until four just doing this stuff," said Wynton.

Then Mark came in to adjust the mikes.

"Wynton, will you move back another foot, please," requested Steve.

Then Steve and Tim joined Mark in the studio. They all fidgeted with the mikes and wires.

"Okay, let's check this out," Wynton said, meaning a short tune he wrote in one sitting the previous night. "Actually, the piece is going to start with Veal."

Wynton's father's head appeared on the other side of the window while everyone was making these microphone adjustments. He was flying home to New Orleans that afternoon. Veal and Homey had played on a recording he'd done the day before. He called them his old rhythm section, because they played with him in New Orleans before they came out with Wynton. And J. had also done something that day with E.—Ellis—one of their duets. E. had just performed the music for an animation that also featured Yo-Yo Ma. When Ellis made a recording with Wynton, *Resolution of Romance*, he said, "I was sideman to my son," when people asked him about it.

In the studio, as fussing with the mikes continued, Ellis left before father and son could say goodbye to each other.

Billy Banks walked in just as he went. Billy had checks for the musicians, including the engineers, for their recording work at the Vanguard.

In the control room a few minutes later to make a phone call, Wynton could overhear Rob complaining to Matt about his check.

"I left the Vanguard at five A.M.," said Rob. "That means I was there fourteen hours, counting from when I came in to help with the setup. *They* get paid overtime, but not me." By "they" he meant the Sony people. There, in the studio, Rob had no official duties and left shortly to search for another of the books he wanted to add to his collection. A voracious reader, Rob liked to buy first editions for his home library while reading a paperback copy of the book so the first edition wouldn't become worn. He'd been looking lately for Malraux's *Picasso's Mask*, which a store outside the city said it would sell him for seventy-five dollars if he couldn't find a cheaper copy in town.

The night I first met Rob in Houston, he and some of his boys came to my gig. They were dressed in the highest and finest style. They began talking about how they would whup my behind in ball. I went to their neighborhood still in my suit to spank their asses on their home court. After the game, Rob drove me to his house. Still sweating, grey suits soaked, we turned in by this big old house, and I'm thinking Rob is a spoiled Little Lord Fauntleroy whose hobby is jazz. He keeps going past the big place to this garage in the back. His apartment is basically one room. One tiny room. That's where he lived. But what was in that room—I wasn't ready for that. Nothing but books, records, and CDs. Thousands of them. And bad shit too. Thomas Mann, Ellison, Ellington. Damn. Bird. Hindemith. Hemingway. That room had a vibration in it. Seeing all those books and records of Rob's, it made me want to cry. Just the solitude and loneliness of that type of intellectual engagement for a young Afro-American. I said to myself, if this man can know all this music and literature, he can surely learn how lights and microphones work. And that's how I hired him. Now he knows more about lighting and sound at a jazz gig than anyone in the world. Musicians in other bands have called him our eighth man.

Back in the studio, the band worked on the section after the first bridge in the new tune, which Wynton had yet to name. In a tune using the standard form of thirty-two measures or bars, the bridge was the third section of eight bars, linking the first two so-called A sections of eight bars each with the last, eight-bar repeated section of A. The bridge in that form was called the B section.

In this tune, however, the form had been stretched, so that after the introduction, the first two sections, and the bridge, instead of returning to an A section there were variations on the form, with another bridge, and so on. The musicians had to see this, hear this, for any single part of the tune to sound right when they recorded it. In that sense, context was everything: first, the context of the old form the band was taking off from; second, the context of the overall changed form, which still had a fundamental relationship to the classic AABA form.

And the parts everyone was reading were just a guide. Within those parts there was not only room for improvising but the expectation of it. *It's a little like what a doctor in an emergency room might do. He or she has been trained and will be working with other people, also trained. They all have experience. And there is a form to what they do, say, for example in setting a broken leg. But when that doctor comes in to work, he or she doesn't really know what kind of broken leg will need fixing or exactly how it will need to be fixed. So there's a good deal of freedom within the form. In fact, a doctor who goes only by the book in unplanned situations will probably not be a good doctor.*

A better analogy is language. Everyone uses it. There are ways to respond to questions, patterns to convey thoughts, and so on, yet the exchange of ideas and feelings in words really takes place among people with the free-flowing improvisation of language. The impact grows when a poet uses the language creatively. Language then becomes high art. It leaves a deeper impression if you take the time to check it out.

When a band was playing jazz, the process of improvisation was constantly evolving, within the context of everything else it was doing. Musicians who didn't understand this might still be good improvisers but that wouldn't make them good jazz musicians.

Now, as Wynton's band rehearsed this section of the new piece, Veal had a suggestion.

"I could do it faster than that," he said.

"Okay," Wynton replied. "Let's go again from the same place."

They did.

"Okay, let's go from the bridge to the solo."

That took a few seconds.

"Okay, now from J.'s solo."

All this time the engineers were adjusting their dials in the control room. The band still hadn't recorded anything.

"Okay, let's do a take," said Wynton. "Anyone want to do the form again? Okay, we'll do the form and then take a take."

Sandy Palmer, another engineer, walked into the studio to supervise the raising and lowering of the ceiling panels, which affected the sound. She touched a button and entire portions of the ceiling went up or down. The band continued its preparations.

"We can't have the parts coming in like they weren't related," Wynton said. "Veal, you got to play like it was a spiritual. Okay, let's do a take."

"Stand by," Steve said. "Take One. 'And the Band Played On.'"

"No, that's not what tune it is."

"What is it?"

"It's called . . . 'Brother Veal,'" Wynton said, giving it a name finally, on the spot. Eventually this would fill out the rest of the recording of *Blue Interlude*.

"Okay."

"Brother Veal" took about three minutes to play.

"Great!" said Steve when it was finished.

"Let's go check it out," Wynton announced to the musicians. And they put their instruments down and went into the control room to listen to what they had just created. Wynton sat next to Steve, in front of the panel of dials, with two huge speakers standing beyond them, in front of the window to the studio.

"J., I want you to play a direct call-and-response."

"Okay, Mister Skain," he said, with mock solemnity. "Yass sir."

While the men were listening and talking, a piano tuner worked in the studio, making fine adjustments. Sometimes J. would ask a tuner to de-tune a piano he thought had been worked on too much.

"I think the form is not . . . how long is it, Steve?" asked Wynton.

"Three minutes, nineteen seconds."

Warm Daddy and Swing Doom made suggestions to improve the piece. Wynton encouraged that. The two players knew their own instruments better than Wynton did. Their ideas could also make the music better. Wynton didn't accept everything the men suggested. But he was always making improvements and changes himself. Usually when he changed something more than once he went back to what it was to begin with.

"Okay, I got another part for that bridge." And Wynton sang it to the men.

"All right, so here's what we're going to do. I'm going to run down the form one more time. We got to hit that F major chord together or it sounds nebulous. Another thing. We can play horn parts through Veal's solo."

It was just after two o'clock. The band went back into the recording room to rehearse what it had just discussed.

"I want a sound of complete contrast," Wynton said to Veal about his bowing at the beginning, which Veal admitted he was not completely comfortable with. *He's not really comfortable with bowing, period. He makes a big fuss about it. But it will be cool. Veal's a perfectionist. He's as fussy about getting his bowing right as he is about looking clean before we go on stage. From the way he talks, he's like this at home in Atlanta, too. I haven't been to his crib there. But to hear him talk about it, you can picture it. For one thing, he plays the drums, too, and he's been setting up a special room for that in his house.*

"I'm crying," he says. "Crying to see my baby at home." Veal is one of the world's great romantics. He loves to play ballads, sweet music, put his mattress out on the balcony in the summertime and enjoy a down-home experience.

Swing Doom.

"Okay, let's do another take."

Take 2

Wynton: "If I get lost, let's all get lost together."

Take 3

"Bravo!" Steve exclaimed.

Take 5

Wynton: "Okay, let's try Cone's tune now."

Take 17

It was beginning to get late; almost nine-thirty P.M. The band had had a break for lunch, another for dinner. It was ten hours since the musicians had started and they were still trying to get another tune Wynton had just written a new version of, "Sometimes It Goes Like That." It was in his head when he woke up that morning. *I never have to force a tune. It just comes out.*

"Sometimes It Goes Like That" was about seven minutes long; "Brother Veal" was three, Cone's tune was about five. That made about fifteen minutes of music on a CD that would need to be around sixty-five or seventy. Fifteen minutes in ten hours; that was about a minute and a half per hour, average, music to recording time. Of course that included the breaks, but studio time costs the same whether the musicians are eating lunch or recording.

If this were a symphony orchestra, the players would be in their second or third day of recording, based on the time they'd spent. A typical orchestra can go two sessions a day, maybe two and a half hours per session, maximum. And unlike this jazz band an orchestra is paid overtime. But the band is paid much more per day to record.

It was too late to start another tune. The band would do a couple more takes, and then J. and Wynton were supposed to record something they'd missed doing a few weeks ago. The band would have to record *Blue Interlude* the next day.

Take 21

Another nice day. What would he be doing if he weren't here again this morning? J. and Wynton had stayed in the studio until after midnight and Wynton was up early making plans. *How is the band going to get through this shit?* It was a question that wouldn't be asked in the studio, where the only obligation Wynton felt was to get the music out. *And go on to the next thing.* He worked on one thing at a time, but he juggled dozens of projects.

Why hadn't the band been able to play "Sometimes It Goes Like That"? The men had played an earlier version of it on tour. And they'd worked on it yesterday, late afternoon

Jazz in the Bittersweet Blues of Life

and early evening, several hours total.
puzzled.

He called Mike Basden in the morning and a. meet him in the studio to go over the parts. Mike use. in school with Delfeayo at Berklee. He'd been helping Wy. ton with letters and copying parts. A lot of the mail Wynton received was requests for autographs and pictures and Mike helped him with that. He made up some stationery with a trumpet on it, and he'd been writing notes on that. But Wynton read everything that came in. Sometimes he wrote letters. Mainly he talked on the phone or with people when they came to a gig. He'd give someone his phone number just after he'd met them, especially someone who wanted to play and who might come to New York. Or it might be a child. Wynton would tell him, "Call me if I'm ever in town," and five years later he would and they'd get together. He gave his private, unlisted numbers to so many people that his manager regularly had to get him a new, "private" number for personal business.

People called him at all hours. From everywhere. He had voice mail, too, but he never checked the messages. No one answered the phone for him, though.

He might play a trick when someone called him.

"Is Wynton there?"

"That's him."

Or he might say, "E. Dankworth." E. Dankworth is an obscure English trumpet player whom J. discovered and used on one of his recordings, *Deep in the Shed*. According to the credits, he played on two tunes, one of which J. named after him.

"You're changing the voicing here?" Mike Basden asked about a passage in "Sometimes It Goes Like That." Voicing

... red to the instrumentation—for example, one voicing would call for the notes to be played by tenor saxophone and trumpet; another for trombone. You could play the same thing twice but with different voicings and it would change the whole sound, the whole feeling of the music.

"All right, Basden, I'm just going to put it in parentheses here." Later, Mike would erase Wynton's pencil marks and correct the part in ink. He had a neat hand. Wynton's was very tidy—small precise markings and the erasures were all clean. Some passages needed playing again and again, and Wynton always tried things to see how they sounded, but a lot of the music just went straight down on the paper the way it sounded in Wynton's head and never got changed. Eventually, the parts would be inputted on a computer, a system that Wynton would perfect with Ronnie Carbo, Mike's successor. But Wynton always wrote the first version of his music by hand. That never changed.

Mike marked the other changes Wynton showed him. Warm Daddy wandered in, a cup of coffee in one hand and a cigarette in the other. Wynton didn't say anything and neither did Wess. Wynton never talked idly when he was in the studio. Working or not, he'd visit with people when he was home, where they were constantly stopping by at all hours. But not here. It was too easy to lose his concentration.

Wess kept walking around while Mike and Wynton kept working.

But Wess's being in the room had changed the vibe. Wess never yelled or made any kind of violent motion with his body. He didn't squeeze your hand hard like Cone or Homey or Swing Doom. He just *was*. There. His presence. You could be anywhere with him and you'd sense it. Just shopping in a mall, where he liked to check out the fashions. He'd be walking along in his Bermuda shorts, with the matching shirt that had a print of some golfers on it. And a straw hat. Wess never hurried when he walked. It was like he enjoyed each step, which was the way he was on the bandstand, always taking the music a phrase at a time, basking in it. *You never push Wess. He gets there. Yes indeed.*

"Warrrrm Daddy!"

"See? Here. I put trombone A natural," Wynton said to Mike. "You put A flat. Gotdammit."

While Mike puzzled over this Wess went to the piano to tune his alto sax.

"See right here? Measure twelve. Who you giving the melody to?"

"Uh-huh."

"Don't see how you could misunderstand that. No, wait a second, that's my fault, it's incomprehensible what I wrote there."

"Yeah, Skain, well, that's what I'm talking about. How the fuck is someone supposed to do his job when he gets shitty directions like that?"

Mike was skinny. Quiet. Smoked cigarettes. He was good company usually, but when he made mistakes at a moment like this it really bothered Wynton. He felt he had to watch him, which only made Mike more angry.

"They're all kind of misprints in here, man," said Wynton, annoyed. How many were Mike's fault? How many Wynton's changes? Whatever the correct answer, the one thing that made Wynton angry in a pressured situation was having to explain things more than once—that, and someone's being defensive.

"Man, I got to concentrate on the trumpet part today. And instead we're dealing with this!"

some good swing

"That's the part I asked you about, Skain."

"You got to pay attention!"

Wynton was getting on a vibe with Mike. He looked at him by just raising his eyes from the music he was staring down at and cracked a little smile.

Silence in the room, except Sandy and Mark fussing with wires and mikes.

"Mike, this one is my fault here. This is a whole tone scale here. I'll correct this now. This is my fault. I didn't write in the accidentals."

Accidentals are sharps and flats—without them, Mike could not guess what Wynton meant to write.

"You got the soprano part?"

"No, Skain. You told me not to write it out."

"But for this spot right here . . . Okay, where'd you get *this* from, bruh? Where'd you see that? You go up to a C. I don't see where you got that note from."

"It should have been an A."

"You have a B. Measure seven, that's the part I had to change. You have those parts?"

"Not yet."

"I want you to hurry up and do that. I want to work on that when the cats all get here." Wynton stared at the parts, his chin in his right hand, his pencil in his writing hand, which was his left. The piano could fall off its legs and he wouldn't notice.

"Steve, could you play the last takes from yesterday? Thanks, Steve."

"Wess, you are not going to play that solo. Todd is."

"Any particular reason, bruh? You don't like what I'm playing, Skain?"

"No, I just rethought how I wanted it played. And I like this form here, in J.'s part. That's a terrible spree."

"It has to happen fast, those shifts," said Wess. "And there has to be a feeling. You're combining so many different elements."

The part they were talking about grew out of a chance encounter the previous day. Wynton was at the piano during a break, Wess heard something and played it. Wynton elaborated. Once they had the nucleus, the concept, the melody, then they added some devices, made it into some blues, gave it a form. And it became a tune the band often played. Sometimes it went like that: you got the first motif and built around it.

When all the musicians were in the studio, they reviewed the corrections. They didn't like learning a piece like this, in the studio, but there was no alternative because the studio time had been booked. What was important was not to panic. Wynton never panicked because he was certain everything would come out all right. *Early afternoon, we still have* Blue Interlude *but you can't panic. Then nothing will get done and you'll feel like shit, too. Anyway, it's just a piece of music, not a war.*

Finally around one-thirty P.M. the band played its first take of the day, which lasted about two minutes. *Damn, the shit sounds good.*

"May I make a suggestion?" asked Steve. "The sixteenth notes could be more accented. Also, did you want the articulation to be matched?"

Steve asked many questions like that. A Hofstra graduate, he used to play the violin. He and Wynton started working on Wynton's recording for trumpet and strings, *Hot House Flowers*, back in 1984. That was Wynton's second jazz recording. Tim has been with Wynton since his debut jazz recording. Tim and Steve didn't panic either. They knew Wynton would not undermine them, that he had complete faith in what they were doing. Nor could he do their job. *Some people make you think*

*they could a better job than you. If that's true, then let's see.
Otherwise, they should shut the fuck up.*

Shut.

The.

Fuck.

Up.

"No, I don't want those notes articulated. I want everyone to play them with their own expression."

"Wynton, why don't you come in and listen to it."

"Is it all right?"

"There are a couple of things that don't seem tight."

"You all want to take a break or do it again?"

The men voted to break. Wynton and Steve listened in the control room. Most of the men joined them, even though they didn't have to. *We're all concerned about how a recording goes. We don't walk around every day listening to our own music, but the cats feel that what we are doing is important. We know that we're maintaining the feeling of jazz and passing the tradition to the next generation. All the encores, the performances for teachers and students, the sold-out concerts, tell us jazz fans identify with what we are doing too. We want to make recordings that speak to these people, that justify their support for all these many years.*

"You should have kept swinging, Veal."

"Uh-huh."

While they listened and talked, J. checked takes from last night.

"We're not playing with enough of a vibe," Wynton said. "And we need to get a take with a good solo from Wess."

Half a dozen takes later, the musicians switched to one more new tune, "Reaching for the Stars." Maybe it was the hour, maybe something else, but everyone sounded tired. Perhaps the tune was too hard. To keep up with his enormous creative output, Wynton went into the studio like this at least two or three times a year with the whole band. He did a few other sessions on his own, a tune for Branford, something for Teresa Brewer, Shirley Horn. And for more than a decade he'd made at least one more classical recording annually, so he averaged several CDs a year. No other serious musician put out this much original work.

The band had more sessions scheduled but they were for other works. *One thing is, when we do a record we do it. No waiting around for a year to get it. We go into the studio for two days, we have a record.*

We were going to have one now. Blue Interlude.

Take 31

Albert Murray had appeared. He'd entered the control room while the band was trying to learn "Reaching for the Stars" and now he was going with the men to a Brazilian restaurant for dinner. But he wasn't eating. He was just coming along. He looked grand in his seersucker jacket. Still teaching at seventy, and writing a new book, a new novel.

Al is tough, but he's sweet. I've been going to see him since the early 1980s. Learning from him. On some Sunday morning or late night weekday, I visit him and ask about all sorts of things. Or he stops by at my apartment. He never calls to say he's coming. Like now, at the studio, there he was.

Murray didn't stay long. He had to get home. He was on a schedule finishing his novel. A routine.

It was Al who taught me that jazz musicians have artistic objectives that are functional. He teaches me a little more of that each time I see him. Context and meaning. And it's amazing, he used to be in the Air Force. For many years. The Air Force and art. He's been married to the same lady all these

years. Mozelle. Radiant. She sometimes comes with him to our
gigs, gives us words of encouragement and an annual fruitcake.

Murray left the restaurant before the others finished their meal, and Wynton left too, even though Rob's order hadn't come yet. Rob would deal with the check. Then he was going back to the hotel to watch a baseball game on television. Everywhere the band traveled Rob wanted to watch baseball. People gave him tickets. Once, at a truck stop in Arizona, Rob met a driver who was taking a delivery to San Diego for a game and he said to call him anytime we wanted tickets. But there was never time to go to a game. So Wynton and Rob and Cone and Homey played catch. They bought some baseballs and gloves and a bat, along with a football and basketball, which they kept in a big bag and took on the bus. That was how Rob met that driver in Arizona; they were waiting for Harold to get a permit, because the bus was crossing the state border from Utah to Arizona, and they were playing catch in a huge parking lot with mountains in the distance and the Grand Canyon nearby, though you couldn't see that. It was hot, too. And Rob met the baseball fan from San Diego.

Back in the studio it was not yet six, which was when the musicians were supposed to return.

Mike was photocopying corrected parts for *Blue Interlude*. When was he going to be finished? Did anyone know?

The men started drifting back.

"Come on. We got serious work to do.

"Let's play with extreme fire and passion."

"Skain?" asked J. "Does that mean we can play how we feel?"

"Yeah."

"Good." And he banged the piano very hard. Everyone laughed.

"Okay. *Blue Interlude*."

"Take thirty-one," said Steve. "Rolling."

"Hold it, bruh," said Veal. "There's a click on the bass. Okay. That's okay."

Take 32

"Take thirty-two. Rolling."

Wynton couldn't stop laughing.

Take 34

The room seemed transformed, and everyone in it, as if suddenly the men had simultaneously sensed what they were doing, as though the pent-up energy of the long day, and the day before, and the week before that, were exploding, there, in that room, with that music. Wynton danced during passages when he wasn't playing. *It's good we haven't rehearsed this again, or too much of the swing might have leaked away during the rehearsal.* The band played through the entire piece, all forty-plus minutes of it, and when the musicians were done Steve hollered, "Bravo!" and they played the whole thing again, again without stopping.

What time is it?

What do we do tomorrow?

Where will be?

These were questions to which Wynton had no answers. Lost in the world of Sugar Cane and Sweetie Pie, the two "mythic lovers" whose story *Blue Interlude* tells in music, lost in the long duet, the battle royale, that Wess and Todd play about two-thirds of the way through the piece, and then the ballad that follows, lost in the warmth and depth of that sound, Wynton made eye contact with Homey. *He knows. I watch Todd's body, the way he plays with his whole body, I remember the boy I met in St. Louis who said can I get out my saxophone and now here he is a man, listen to what he is dealing with! Todd Williams, who doesn't curse, practices each night in his room, calls his wife every day when we're on the road, never comes unprepared. And whose father makes the best barbecue anywhere that we always enjoy when we're in St. Louis. The last time at Todd's folks' house there must have been I don't know how many people enjoying that Williams family food, that hospitality, that love that you can hear now in Todd's music.*

After a break the band rehearsed and recorded Todd's *Jubilee Suite*. Wynton was beginning to feel the effects of having just five hours of sleep the night before. Or maybe it was the cold he'd had the previous day, which had gone away like he knew it would. *A cold, five hours of sleep, and more work.*

Deadline for a Dance

"Wynton! Wynton?"

"Yes, Mr. Garth. Yes sir."

It was Garth Fagan calling.

Garth Fagan was from Rochester, where Wynton had met him after a gig in the late 1980s, when he was still feeling depressed about his brother leaving his band. Garth saw him walking along the street, stopped his car, and gave him a ride. They drove to Garth's studio, where the choreographer introduced Wynton to his dancers.

"This is Wynton Marsalis and he's already a mean dude and someday he's going to be meaner." They put on an entire performance for Wynton. He had never forgotten that. They'd kept in touch.

So Wynton and Garth Fagan became close, and one day he asked Wynton to write a piece for him. He called it *Griot New York*. In Africa, a griot was a storyteller, a kind of oral historian of his people's culture.

Garth shared with Wynton a poem he had written. The poem expressed the concept of the ballet that he envisioned. About the actual story, Wynton talked to Al Murray, who told him it was about three things: the city, the people in the city, and what those people do in the city.

The premiere's projected date was a year away.

After six months or so Garth started calling him. How was Wynton doing? Wynton told him it was cool.

Then, in the fall, just after Wynton returned from South America, he called a friend and asked how long it took to choreograph a ballet.

Garth had just called him again in Mexico and reminded Wynton that the premiere was just three months away. And Wynton still didn't have any music to send him.

Wynton's friend said he didn't know much about choreography. Creative time was always impossible to calculate. And of course there was a relationship to how long the projected ballet was. But certainly just the physical work of blocking out all those moves and coordinating them, never mind their aesthetic coherence and impact, certainly for a work as ambitious as Garth's a few months, minimum, would be necessary. Wouldn't it?

It's better to work this way. When you are making something, you just go. With what you felt first. Then you back over it, make it sing, make it lyrical. As long as you have the form. The form for Garth was all there, even though he ended up not using each part. Sometimes it goes like that. The piece came out longer than anything I had ever written. Two hours of music with some very unusual forms. But late. Very late.

three

I can see her standing outside the window while we're rehearsing. It's Sunday morning. We arrived in Snowmass yesterday afternoon. Bright sun, sky an incredibly pure blue, still some snow on the ski slopes that start behind our hotel. We're rehearsing Armstrong. She has red hair and is wearing black sunglasses, and she's holding a little girl in her arms. The window is open, but I imagine she could hear this good hot swing even if it weren't. Several people stand near her, and others walk by, on their way from the shops to the hotel, or from the hotel to the shops. Except she's not shopping. She's dancing. Like a little girl herself.

standards & riffs

1. Improvisation under Christmas Tree

Lights off on the Christmas tree. Was it late at night or early in the morning?

All those days after we got back from rehearsals or recordings, continuing to work on the parts. Lost in the indulgent obsession of making the imagined, the invisible, and inaudible, physical.

Then it was done. A big performance that you've been working to get ready for a long time, a packed auditorium, everyone dressed so fine, lots of stories in the newspapers. The strain of nerves that only attends a premiere. Something being born. The sense of everyone pulling together to surmount the inevitable glitches and unforeseen problems of the untested, untried. The triumphant wave of many emotions at the final curtain. Bows, flowers, and kisses for all. Then it's over. The world stops, but it continues. You have to figure out how to get back on. Same headlines, same intrigues, same personal problems.

Nobody even stopped you in the street to say, "Hey, man, saw the show. Yeah." After all of that. Damn. In the bittersweet blues of life. That's truly a homecoming. My boy Westray says if you want to be messed over, just go back to where you're from.

Is it morning or night?

Lights off on the tree, gifts and cards scattered on the carpet that had recently been replaced. Every now and then the loneliness catches you. Whew! I don't know.

You spent years of time alone in a practice room, or over an empty piece of paper, struggling to blacken it with some sound or idea that will live. And your motives were not always pure. Maybe it was to become recognized by a girl you wanted. Or to escape a social condition you abhorred. Or for applause of an audience. Could be just the profanity of personal pleasure with your own skills. In any case these things are never free. The only free thing is the idea. And when you get the girl, someone loses the girl. When you leave one social condition, there's another. When the audience claps, they stop. When you lavish love on yourself, you can't love others. Then it comes to you. To do the thing you love because you love it. Then the outrage of a competitive musician, the tirades of a spurned lover, the barbs of the offended critic, the self-indulgent narcissism of artistic prerogative, and even the condemnation of a corrupted culture are consumed by the art itself. That's why we can still enjoy Duke's Such Sweet Thunder, *having no idea of what surrounded its creation. Was it on time? Did the critics like it? Anyway, the overwhelming joy of having lovers, and critics, and compositions, of having fans, students, die-hard friends, personal dramas, not to mention a great band of musicians, to* discover the world with, cannot be expressed with words. To listen to the sound of Wess Anderson, the J. Master, Veal, every night. Homey. Thank you. Cone.

I have been playing or hanging out in clubs damn near since I was born. Dance halls, juke joints, jazz clubs, concert halls, you name it. All kinds of shit goes on. People come in clean as the board of health and others come raggedy, drunk, make a fool out of themselves, and bring life to the party. You read the papers about this and that star who was seen out here and there with this one and that one. Well let me tell you something, most of the people who go out all the time in discos and bars are amongst the unhappiest and loneliest motherfuckers in the whole world. If you want to be happy, go inside. Inside yourself. Inside the people you love. Inside your art. Inside seems much lonelier than outside. Don't be fooled. You go in far enough, it's always warm and good.

A holiday like Christmas makes you go home, go inside. It brings all that shit you run from right to you. Stuff slows down. I miss my boys.

Here's a picture of me and my great-uncle, the stonecutter. He was born in 1880 something. Had a little shotgun house on Governor Nicholls Street in New Orleans. Look at the vibe he's on, the way he had his hand on my shoulder. He listened to the radio every morning, got up around five-thirty, liked black strong hot coffee. Aggravated the hell out of my great-aunt. But loved her. He loved me too. Old man, always having stubble on his face, wanting you to kiss him. Would take me around to the barber shop and show off how smart I was. This was in the 1960s. He didn't like Muhammad Ali because he changed his name from Cassius Clay. Wouldn't fight in Vietnam and was always bragging. Couldn't understand why we loved our Afros. "Boy, when you going to cut all that damn hair?" Couldn't understand bell-bottom jeans. "Son, women wore those kind of

pants in the 1920s." Hey, I loved Muhammad Ali. I loved my
uncle too. He was truly old-school. You know what really was a
trip about him? Here's this tough-ass stonecutter, grew up in
the sho-nuff south, and was known not to take shit off white
folks back when that could cost you more than an ass-whipping.
And his favorite TV show was Lawrence Welk. That used to
blow my mind. Didn't like Muhammad, but wanted to watch
Lawrence damn Welk. And still was as soulful as somebody
could be. That's why my daddy used to tell me, "You never
know about somebody unless you know." My great-uncle had a
nickname for me too, and he was the only one who used it. He
called me Punny. I called him Pomp.

Sometimes when I read one of these articles, or someone will
come up disrespecting me from some misimpression they got
from somewhere, I remember what's real. I remember the name
my uncle gave me, remember the scrubgrass underfoot in the
cemeteries where they put his stones, how the people in New
Orleans had to be buried above ground because the city was be-
low sea level. Remember Pep's barber shop, and me and Pomp
walking hand in hand past the big brown faded Luzianne Coffee
sign on the wooden side of a neighborhood watering hole.

Voices in my head, improvising images of my life:

Wynton Watches Parade

NEW YORK—Jazz and classical trumpet player
Wynton Marsalis took his sons, Wynton Jr. and
Simeon, to Macy's famed Thanksgiving Day parade. The children sat one at a time on their father's shoulders to see the bands and floats that
came marching down Fifth Avenue.

Marsalis said he was always going to parades as
a boy in New Orleans where he grew up.

"It's not the same in New York. But who doesn't love a parade?"

Late night.

After a brief break the band came back to rehearse the Fagan piece, which Wynton had finally completed. Except Mike Basden's successor, Ronnie Carbo, who went home for only a day or so because he was working on the parts for the ballet. When the parts arrived everyone got busy right away because Wynton called a rehearsal for that night, which was a Sunday, and the next day the band went into the studio again to start recording, and the musicians had rehearsals with Garth, too, and then of course the premiere.

That was the weekend when Garth explained a decision about the choreography for the ballet. Because of time constraints, he would only be able to choreograph part of the piece and would create another work from other Wynton tunes. Outwardly, Wynton wasn't bothered. The music would survive on recording.

Carbo and Wynton went out to the Brooklyn Academy of Music to watch the dancers rehearse. It was Saturday, the day before the band members came back from New Orleans, and Atlanta, and Albany, New York, where Pine Cone had visited a friend, who was studying engineering there.

"We can't do it, Wynton," said Garth. "Not the whole thing."

Fagan Finally Nixes Numbers

NEW YORK—Choreographer Garth Fagan had to lower the boom on his musical collaborator Wynton Marsalis, whose original score for *Griot New York* came in too long and too late.

Fagan is a Jamaican native whose group, Garth Fagan Dance, has been located since 1970 in Rochester, New York. *Griot* is a production of the Brooklyn Academy of Music's New Wave Festival, with sets and costumes by Martin Puryear.

Marsalis reportedly did not begin work in earnest on his commissioned composition until his septet toured Europe two months before the premiere.

"I'm disappointed," he said upon hearing Fagan's decision.

The complete Marsalis score employs a variety of jazz techniques to recreate a kind of dance kaleidoscope. There is a fox trot, a waltz, a calypso, and so on, in music that would take two hours to perform without a break.

"I like to have fun with the old forms," Marsalis said. "But they're just a takeoff point.

"What matters is people," he continued. "The best thing about jazz is its interest in human relationships."

What could Wynton say to him? "I understand." That's all he could say, except he added, "You got to promise me one thing, Garth. Someday we're gonna hook it up and do the whole thing. The *whole* thing."

"Wynton. Wyn-ton." *That told me what I needed to know.* "I'm not mad that you were late. I know you worked hard. Of course, Wynton."

"We are our music," Marsalis reportedly told his septet before the premiere.

"So, play with intensity. With feeling and with urgency. Keep your concentration up. Don't worry about little mistakes. Get into the actuality of who we are and let's play the way we want to play."

The group recorded the entire two-hour work in the BMG studios the same week there were rehearsals with the dancers, preceding the premiere. The work was then performed on three consecutive nights.

The Marsalis group remained in New York for a Christmas program before leaving for an out-of-town engagement. The group returned to New York in mid-December for another Christmas program and another day in the studio. Still not satisfied with the quality of the playing on the recording, Marsalis flew the septet back to New York at his own expense just before the new year for one more recording session. The group then remained in New York for a prior, one-night engagement, following which a rare vacation was scheduled for all except Marsalis.

Though he had promised his manager to take some time off, Marsalis instead devoted several weeks to learning the repertoire for a recording of twentieth-century trumpet and piano music. In addition, Marsalis spent his time away from the band sitting in for a protégé, Nicholas Payton, in a recorded session of New Orleans music led by Dr. Michael White at the Village Vanguard. Marsalis also played several sets at the Blue Note as part of that New York club's birthday celebration for Dizzy Gillespie, whom Marsalis reveres for his musicianship, creativity, encouragement of musicians around the world, and general love of life.

During preparations for the classical recording sessions, held in Princeton, New Jersey, Marsalis visited the Providence, Rhode Island, home of his former Juilliard piano teacher and fellow Tanglewood alumnus, Judy Stillman. Stillman was the pianist on the recording. While rehearsing, they drove together to Boston, where composer and former New England Conservatory president Gunther Schuller coached Marsalis in the proper tempi and interpretation for several of the works.

Upon their return to Providence for more rehearsing, Marsalis dropped the new C trumpet that David Monette had just built for him, bending the leadpipe so severely that he had to telephone Monette in Chicago to please come and repair it. Marsalis had himself only recently traveled to Chicago to pick the horn up and "play-test" it. Monette flew immediately to Providence, where he joined the two musicians and stayed overnight at Stillman's home.

Late night, voices in my head.
The phone on the piano rang.
Wynton picked it up with one hand and the C trumpet with the other. He began playing a section of the Shostakovich First Piano Concerto, which is virtually a double concerto for trumpet and piano. He was supposed to be recording it with Emanuel Ax in London but he had cancelled the

gig because he didn't feel he was ready. They would try to do it another time.

Wynton put the trumpet down.

"E. Dankworth."

It was his partner on the phone. Anyone he knew or was working with might be his partner.

Todd Williams had been calling, too. He was returning to the band after some time off. He and his wife had moved to New York, where she was going back to graduate school, and the Deacon was going back on the road with the band. He was even going on the Duke Ellington tour at the end of the year as a member of the Lincoln Center Jazz Orchestra. During his break he had volunteered in one of the St. Louis schools as a clarinet teacher.

When the news of his coming back got out in the band, Wess called Wynton up one night.

"Williams," Wess said. That was all. Then he hung up.

It was difficult telling Todd's replacement, but Wynton had done it with others before and he knew he'd have to do it again someday, maybe someday soon. *All you can do in your dealings with other people is say the truth. Kindly. It'll work out. Cats when you tell them, they know. They might not act or talk like it right away, but they do know. They do.*

Now, packing, there was too much stuff in the bag with his music in it. How was he going to get all this ready before the ride came? A snapshot fell out of the bag. Wynton embracing a woman who had come backstage to greet him. A stranger. She'd sent it to him in the mail. There was nothing sexual about the embrace. It was just a momentary expression on someone else's part of the human need to touch.

Voices . . .

Dress Rehearsal

BROOKLYN—After a long joint rehearsal, preceded by a separate recording session for the band and stage rehearsal for the dancers, Wynton Marsalis's tour manager informed the Marsalis septet they should come dressed up for the next day's *Griot New York* dress rehearsal.

"Bring your vines," Lolis Elie told the men. "We may be on television."

"Says who?" asked Mr. Marsalis. "Nobody checked with me. So don't bring your suits. I'm tired of this TV shit and all these interviews and everything. No disrespect to you, Brother Elie."

Later, as the septet's van returned to Manhattan, Reginald "Swing Doom" Veal and Herlin "Homey" Riley began a song in prayer for Mr. Elie.

Members of the septet included road manager David "Sugar Rob" Robinson in their medley. Sugar Rob, alias Toon, Toon Yab Scab, and Sugar, apparently urged the men to wear suits, too.

"Oh Rob he was hot today," the men sang, in reference to Sugar Toon's, Toon Yab Sugar's, whatever—in reference to his quick and some might argue proper but risky response to his boss's displeasure.

"Oh Rob he says we need suits."

Then, when they serenaded Elie, the words were altered to reflect the band's sense of Elie's differing sensibility.

"He's hot too, though he hides it."

The singing degenerated into commentary

about the temptations of playing in a pit orchestra while some of the world's most beautiful dancers moved to your music on a stage only a few feet away.

Wynton packed his DAT player, with tapes of the recorded ballet that his brother Delfeayo had shipped to him. Delf, who was producing this recording in Steve Epstein's usual role, was back in New Orleans now, planning to get a group together and play at a club in the brothers' hometown.

Earlier that day Marsalis and a few of the others avoided being in an automobile accident when their limousine driver was able to maintain his remarkable composure during a dialogue about "puss."

Marsalis had just come from the recording studio, where he and his group's former pianist, Marthaniel Roberts, or Marcus, or just J., were in tears upon completion of the recording of a ballad, "Spring Yaounde," they play in the ballet *Griot New York.*

The ballad seemed to trigger this emotion in all who heard it. Reportedly, the dancers responded the same way when they first heard it, at a rehearsal in Rochester during which the ballad section was composed by Marsalis on the spot.

At the recording of the ballad there was just one take and then Marsalis put his horn down and Roberts said, "I guess we got that one."

Marsalis said, "Lord have mercy."

"Well, that's done. That's it. 'Spring Yaounde.'"

Rushing to reach the Fagan rehearsal on time, the duo left immediately for Brooklyn, with Roberts holding on to Marsalis's arm.

Roberts is blind.

The traffic was very heavy near the bridge over the East River and the pace of the trip was slow. The artists used the extra time to reflect on artistic and other matters.

"That was a glorious moment and we enjoyed it," Mr. J. said in the car. "And now we're going to Brooklyn."

"It's like a good late-night tussle," responded Mr. Marsalis. "Off the record.

"You're hot, and hotter, and it's better, and even better than that. And then it's over. Done. You just bask in the afterglow. Savor it, cause it might be your last time."

The driver pretended not to listen to the men. He kept cracking a smile and then focusing again on his mission, which was to bring the "cats" safely to the Brooklyn Academy of Music.

"Yass," said J.

"Uh-huh," continued Marsalis. "Art Blakey used to say there's only two kinds of pussy. Good. And better."

Mr. Marcus tried to bring the conversation back to art.

"The way the music opens up there, that's the first time I really hear that."

"You have to know the architecture," responded the composer.

"It's a bunch of little climaxes," said J. "And then one real climax."

"Yes, indeed, yes indeed," replied Wynton.

The subject shifted back to sex. "The only thing even the greatest men talk about more than money and themselves is toon yan," said Marsalis.

"You go anywhere, you go to the most august university in the world, where all the professors in a room are discussing a grand unified theory or breaking the DNA code, someone goes into that room and whispers, 'Tail,' and guaranteed they stop their discussion of DNA and start asking 'Where?' and looking all around."

"So," said the J. Master. "We reached those musical heights a little while ago. And now we've descended to this."

"Where else can you go? Less you want to talk about God."

Whom could he have called at this hour?

It's not sex that gets in the way of a relationship with a woman. It's the negotiating that goes on if you both like it. And if y'all love it, watch out.

Bravo

BROOKLYN—Playing in a pit whose floor was set so low they could barely see the front edge of the stage during the premiere of the ballet, the Wynton Marsalis Septet had to stop for prolonged, boisterous applause and cheering after Marsalis and

Marcus Roberts had played the ballad "Spring Yaounde."

Resplendent in black tux, Marsalis remained in his seat near the audience side of the pit, his trumpet poised to continue the next section of music.

Later, at another *Griot* recording session which followed the premiere, the last of the Marsalis musicians did not leave until dawn, when Homey Riley and Skain Marsalis completed their work on a section of the piece called "Buddy Bolden," a fantastic trumpet solo with drum accompaniment.

"You gonna finish it?" Wynton's brother Delfeayo asked from the control room. Patient, calm, cheerful, "Jalf" or "Jelfy" was serving as producer on this recording.

"Fuck yeah. But I can't be waiting for you to get my sound right. That's a waste of time. I've been waiting for y'all to get the trumpet sound recorded right for ten years."

Ronnie Carbo picked up parts from music stands while the brothers pretended to bicker.

Brother Elie began packing the drums. Homey bounced a basketball on the studio's parquet floor.

"I got to play a gig tomorrow," said Marsalis.

"We finished?" asked Riley.

"I'm trying to figure it out, bruh."

Then Herlin passed the basketball to Wynton, who dribbled and faked a shot, turned to see his brother standing by him, and they embraced.

Late night.

Who put this menu in my bag?

"Mulate's. The World's Most Famous Cajun Restaurant."

With the menu was a news clipping of Wynton playing the trumpet for the boys and girls at the Heart of Mary School.

Mulate's was the restaurant where we'd stopped at the suggestion of one of our drivers. Some of the men were sleeping in the bus when we'd arrived, and a few hadn't wanted to disturb their precious rest for some food. But after we'd ordered, Lolis walked out to the parking lot and banged on the bus windows, hollering, "Wake up, men, you don't know what you're missing." There was a big table with the entire band seated, which meant there was more shrimp for Wynton to sample from other people's plates. You didn't ever want to get Wynton at your table when it was a shrimp dinner, unless you didn't like shrimp.

After the dinner he was invited into the kitchen to sign his name on the wall.

That was a day Wynton did two kids' workshops, one of them at the Heart of Mary School. *Man, those kids were cute sitting in their uniforms at little tables in the gymnasium.*

He played "When the Saints Go Marching in."

That was also the day Wynton conducted a workshop at the university where somebody who knew his father showed him a picture of Ellis Marsalis with John Coltrane.

E. always said talent doesn't mean nothing. "What matters is finding a place that can nourish it." That's the tragedy for so many young jazz musicians today. To learn, they also have to provide a healthy environment for themselves to work in. And that's very hard. Damn near impossible.

One of the students at the university workshop that day was wearing a fancy jacket that said PIMPIN' AIN'T EZ.

Son, you could get a million dollar contract with that type of philosophy.

Wynton tried to tell the kids that one of the things that related jazz and democracy was how you overcame the difficulty of getting along with someone who didn't like you or didn't think like you. And disagreement was part of Wynton's ideal of dialogue in democracy, like it was part of the conversation of jazz.

After the workshop at Heart of Mary School everyone adjourned to the gym where Wynton beat High Point in a game of one on one.

"Mr. Marsalis?" one of the students at one of those workshops asked. "Our teacher made us read an article in the paper. Why are they always writing bad things about you, like you're cold, or your music doesn't have any feeling to it?"

Marsalis Shows Classical Side

PRINCETON, NJ—Jazz trumpet player and composer Wynton Marsalis returned to the recording studio for an album of twentieth-century trumpet and piano classical works.

The session, Marsalis's first classical one in several years, was actually held on the campus of Princeton University in Richardson Hall, stone outside, marble and wood in.

I'd broken the first rule of the road: Know who's meeting you and where. I didn't know where we were supposed to be when I got to Princeton for the recording gig with Judy. It was Sunday. I drove down from New York with my main man Dennis Jeter, the one and only sweet Peety Jeety, and then I didn't know where to go.

I would have telephoned Vernon, my manager Ed Arrendell's partner, a New Jerseyite. But I didn't have his number. Tried Ed, but no one answered. Billy Banks didn't know. I was making all these calls from a phone booth in the freezing cold. Finally I reached Swig, who told me the Nassau Inn. There'd be a message from Steve Epstein when I got there.

The campus was fairly quiet during the dreary January days the musicians and engineers were recording. It was cold, the bare ground frozen.

A student passing by Richardson Hall one morning might have heard Marsalis warming up prior to the recording of Honegger's *Interlude*. The sound was just audible outside, while indoors the reverberations were so powerful that the miking for Marsalis's new C trumpet took an extra long time.

"Don't get depressed," pianist Stillman comforted Marsalis after a slightly disappointing Honegger take.

"I don't get depressed," replied Stillman's former Juilliard pupil. "I'm here to do my job."

A few days earlier, Stillman reportedly stayed with Marsalis at his Lincoln Center apartment as they were completing their preparations.

Stillman, a petite woman with tremendous energy and a high, recurrent laugh, answered Marsalis's phone while she lived at the apartment, upbraiding one female caller who seemed upset, thinking Wynton had a woman living with him. Stillman took umbrage at Marsalis's reputed womanizing and took every opportunity to create problems for him in that regard. Marsalis asked her not to answer the phone in such an ambiguous way. She responded by answering, "Platonic pianist."

Later, Stillman escorted Marsalis out of doors, where they were stopped one day near the elevator by an elderly woman who seemed startled by the sight of the interracial couple.

"Excuse us, dear," cooed Judy. "Yes, we're in love. And we're trying to make as many mulatto babies as we can!"

Later, in Princeton, Wynton suggested to Judy that they make love *to* the music. Twentieth-century classical music.

"Let's make it a scratch'n'sniff album," suggested Judy.

During another playback the two scribbled acrostics to one another.

"Win," Judy began. And Wynton completed the word with "tone."

"Wintone."

JUDITH: I don't know, Wynton. We have a couple of places we need to fix ensemble-wise.

WINTONE: Well, we can take a break now. Steve, what do you think we should do? I'm not tired. I'm not even warmed up.

THEY walked downstairs to the control room and listened.

I can't believe that I missed the same passage the same way.

STEVE stopped the tape.

And would you explain to her what happens when you play those high G's?

STEVE started it again.

Good, that sounded like Miles, it had that edge on it. Different parts have different sounds. Some sound like Pops, some like Dizzy. Now, this sounds like Ray Nance.

THEY debated doing it again.

JUDITH: You just like to be controversial. Whatever I say, you disagree. (HE used to sit on my lap in piano class. No matter what we were studying, HE would always play a blues scale somewhere. I gave HIM an A.)
WINTONE: You can't listen to this kind of music for what you want to put in it but for what's there.

THEY listened again. Then THEY walked back upstairs.

JUDITH: That was too strong, like a man and woman, that trumpet thing, that flourish near the end. Yeah, you know what I mean.

SHE studied at Juilliard herself, graduating with both a bachelor's and master's degree at the age of twenty. SHE also won the school's concerto competition. And SHE earned a doctorate in 1982. Now, in addition to teaching piano at Brown, SHE is artist-in-residence and professor of piano at Rhode Island College. SHE has made many recordings, including a line of CDs for children, but this recording with Wynton is HER first for a major label. HE chose HER.

WINTONE: That shit was hard.
STEVE: Would you like to listen?

THEY gathered around the basement table, in front of two speakers, with musical scores and paper spread out before them.

WINTONE: Wow.
JUDITH: Some work to be done.
WINTONE: I feel we're fighting the tempos. And there's too much air in my sound. My sound is so tubey.

[HE meant there was still a breathy sound to the new trumpet, at least in this hall.]

JUDITH: That part there, it's like ragtime. Has to have a swing to it.
JUDITH: We're finished with that piece.
WINTONE: That was hip. It sounded like some blues.
JUDITH: The bonding of the Jew and Negro. And we look exactly alike.
WINTONE: Only with our clothes on.

Sometimes during breaks producer Steve Epstein studied Marsalis's red-pentel notations for the rough takes of an earlier recording. The notes were copious and detailed.

During the sessions, Richardson Hall was of course empty. A piano tuner from Yonkers entered the hall after every break, while the artists convened in the basement for the playbacks. A page-turner was also employed temporarily, until Stillman complained that he kept stepping on her foot.

They played a Ravel transcription that Judy had introduced Wynton to. It was called *Habanera*. Judy had urged Wynton to include it.

> WINTONE: I want to get a dance feeling on this. Like what you might feel if you and your woman were stopped on the street by the sounds of musicians playing at 3 in the morning, when everyone has gone home. Playing for themselves.

JUDY tried a figure on the piano.

> Don't waste it, don't waste it, baby.

THEY played the piece, which was just a few minutes long. The piano part was delicate, the trumpet melody soaring and melancholy.

> Let's take another break. This Ravel takes a lot of control.

THEY remained on stage. From below, STEVE watched THEM on a monitor connected to a video camera on stage.

> Well, ladies and gentlemen. Before we leave, we're going to play some blues for you.

HE picked up his horn and played an introduction, then sang.

> I've got the suburban blues,
> My American Express Platinum card is overdrawn

My Mercedes is in the shop
My therapist is on vacation
And no one understands me
I've got the suburban blues

The chorus went a full twelve bars. Then HE played another on the trumpet.

THEY left together for dinner. STEVE treated.

Wynton, who played briefly in the orchestra at Juilliard, recalled the performance of a symphony whose music he had forgotten to bring with him. So he had to play it by memory, and his memory was faulty. In the very second measure, he came in in the wrong place, and loud. The conductor just stared at him. *I felt like shit.*

It was something that would never happen in jazz. But that didn't make jazz easier. In fact, it made it harder. In a classical performance, when you made a mistake everyone else kept trying to play what they were supposed to and your mistake stood out. But in jazz everyone was supposed to be listening and when you played something they weren't expecting, which happened all the time, they responded, or they should have. This response took training and imagination.

WINTONE: Man, I think this classical recording might do it for me.

[HE found the adjustment, going from jazz to classical, increasingly difficult when he no longer performed classical music. And what was the reward? So much practice, so little response. It meant making music in a vacuum. Still, he loved this music.]

> Attack. It's the same thing for me always, ever since I was in high school. I noticed this when I recorded with Kathleen Battle. My notes always speak late.

[HE meant that in classical music, where a disproportionate emphasis was placed on accuracy, his notes didn't start as cleanly as he wished they would. But the degree to which HE felt HE was off was extremely small. It was akin to the pilot of a jet touching down on a runway several hundred yards wide a few inches from where he intended.]

> STEVE: I disagree.
> And this is a very good performance, this Halsey that we're doing now.

THEY had been back from dinner for a while now. At the downstairs table, WYNTON thumbed through the copies of *World Boxing*, *Ring*, and *KO* that HE'd bought before dinner.

> WINTONE: I'm going to depend on my vibration.

[It's why HE still liked Marvin Gaye: that he depended on his vibe, his feeling. Plus that voice.]

> I can't hear what I'm playing. It all sounds like shit to me.
> STEVE: Just do what you do best.
> WINTONE: OK, Steve. Where's the video camera?

HE pointed to his johnson.

Late night, early morning. Voices in my head like the men in the band playing.

I'm so tired. I should have slept, but then I would have had to wake up.

What's this tennis ball in my bag?

Me and my partner Benny, the tennis coach, went out for dinner one of the nights in Princeton.

Benny brought along a friend, a woman from Colombia.

"What do you do?" she asked me.

"I sell tennis rackets."

"Oh yeah? What's Steffi using now?"

"We had her in a graphite XTS but we're thinking of changing that. We're thinking . . . what is it we're thinking, Benny?"

Bzzzz. The driver rang the doorbell.

We've played gigs in Princeton, too. At the McCarter Theater. One of the world's great presenters, Bill Lockwood, booked the theater. He's retired. It rained the last time we were there, just like it rained the last days of those recording sessions with Judy. We played "You Don't Know What Love Is." Sometimes I can remember particular solos from gigs long ago.

Bzzzz.

It was still raining when we left. A hard, driving rain that didn't stop until we neared New York.

"Uh-huh. Yeah, I'm almost ready."

E.'s looking out the window; that's in the picture by High Point over on the wall there. All I can see is his back and a profile of his head. He has seen so much change. Sometimes I look at that picture and wonder, what is he thinking?

Bzzzz.

Wynton glanced around once more. *Time to get rid of the Christmas tree.*

Bags.

Books.
Almost left behind my horn!

Out the window, the first ferry of the day was bringing commuters across the Hudson River.

Crescent City Interlude

Wynton was born on October 18, 1961. His family lived for several years in a town outside New Orleans called Kenner. His father, who was a pianist, taught school. Wynton was the second oldest; his brother Branford was a year older. There were four more brothers born after Wynton, the last, Jason, not until the family had been living in New Orleans. A friend of Wynton's father's, Al Hirt, gave him a trumpet when he was little, but he didn't really start to play regularly until just before high school. It was a good way to get girls, being able to play the trumpet (or to play anything), and that's why he practiced, or so he likes to say. He was lucky to have good teachers. And his father helped start the New Orleans Center for the Creative Arts, so he was able to study there as well as at his regular high school. He never had free time. He was a pretty good baseball player, a pitcher, but he had to give that up because of his music. By the end of high school he had gigs almost every night, or so it seemed. He missed fifty days of school his senior year. Wynton, Branford, and their friends played funk in a band they called the Creators. They sported Afros and wore platform shoes. *Played loud and had a lot of equipment. Strobe lights and smoke canisters that blew up. We were country!*

All the brothers except Ellis III, a computer professional, and Mboya, who is autistic, play an instrument. Jason's drums and Ellis's piano pretty much took up the front part of the

Marsalis house. It was not a big place. Steps led to a porch with a roof over it. The roof was painted a bluish green.

The thing about that house is I wasn't there much. And now, when I go back to New Orleans, it's not like we have a family reunion. If my daddy's not on the road he's probably working somewhere. He still teaches, as head of jazz at the University of New Orleans. But he plays at clubs, too, places like Snug Harbor. Jazz musicians are out all the time, usually when other people are home. If you want the excitement of going out, stay home. When I was a little boy it was the same. I'd go with my father when he was playing. I'd meet the other musicians. Hear the music. Well, listen to it. Not until later did I begin to hear it.

Snug Harbor was in the Vieux Carre or French Quarter on Frenchmen Street, a few blocks from the Mississippi River. Bourbon Street was down the block, across Esplanade Avenue, and then a couple of streets over. There were still some clubs on Bourbon Street, and Preservation Hall was there, but what was on Bourbon Street more than anything else was T-shirt stores. And the stores spilled right out onto the sidewalk. Many of the T-shirts featured obscene messages. "Suck it in New Orleans." There was a slightly foul smell on the street, which was closed to cars for several blocks. Of course there were bars and beer vendors and a few strip clubs. You could be walking along one of the side streets and look into the door of a bar and there just a few feet from you would be a woman taking her clothes off. There was no jazz being played in those places.

Bourbon Street got crowded. With the weather warm much of the year, the doors and windows of the clubs were open. So you could be on one side of Bourbon Street listening to a band and, coming from the other side, you heard another band. People who came back to New Orleans tended to like Bourbon Street a little better, because on repeat visits they knew what to expect. And what not to expect. So there wasn't the letdown people could feel the first time if they thought they were going to find the old city of jazz legend. And there was an energy there, a raucous energy on busy nights, with the noise level high and people's spirits. But it was all a little programmed, too, like the wildness at Mardi Gras. Wynton never went home for Mardi Gras.

New Orleans is so different from New York. The Big Easy. Everyone laid back, late for everything. Well, in New Orleans the thing itself is late too. In the 1970s, everywhere you went people looked at each other, gave a nod or said what's happening. Now they're too scared in a lot of places. The first time I said hello to a stranger in New York he looked at me like I was a pervert or was going to rob him. People in New York go around looking down; they're moving too fast to look at you. On the subway, people create spaces to look at to avoid seeing anyone else. In the Crescent City, you looked up and ahead and all around you wherever and whenever you wanted to.

Wynton was home once to make a recording with Marcus Roberts. It was actually Marcus's record, and Wynton was just appearing on it. So was his father.

They'd played together the night before at Snug Harbor, all three of them with Jason on the drums. Jason could already play incredibly well but was still working out ways to accompany a soloist. That was something E. or the J. Master knew like it was part of them: playing *with* someone.

Delfeayo was producing J.'s record. Like Branford, he'd studied at Berklee in Boston. And he played the trombone. But Wynton and his brothers didn't generally perform together. The only time the whole family had ever been on the same stage was at Alice Tully Hall to raise money for autism research.

Marcus was making the Marsalis cuts of his record at St. Joseph's Cathedral, in a part of the city past the Superdome on the other side of the interstate that came downtown from the airport. Built in 1844, St. Joseph's has a very large nave. The day of the recording there had begun with an early-morning mass, and then the piano tuner arrived. He was still there when the musicians came. There were two Steinway pianos, because J. and Ellis were going to play some duets.

Wynton played a little basketball before he came over to the cathedral. J. was already there. He was wearing blue jeans and a red knit shirt and shoes—not running shoes but real shoes. And sunglasses. When Wynton came in, J. was playing a Chopin étude. Then he played a Rachmaninoff prelude. Then he segued into some Scott Joplin. Then he played some blues. The acoustics were very live and it sent a shiver down everyone's spine to stand there and listen to J.

It was hot, like it often is in New Orleans, and humid. It had rained hard the night before, then cleared. After the rain it was even hotter and more humid.

Delfeayo and his assistant Patrick were still laying wires for the recording. Most of the equipment had been shipped from New York but something hadn't arrived. Delfeayo was looking all over for it and he couldn't find it. So the musicians couldn't start yet. Delfeayo never seemed to get upset when this kind of thing happened. And Wynton tried not to. What could anyone do? But Wynton only had a little time that day because he had to catch a plane. So he and J. began rehearsing. They talked about the chord progression of the tune they were going to record, "King Porter Stomp."

"There's something about that E flat that's important," said J.

They listened to an old recording of the tune, which was by Jelly Roll Morton.

It felt good playing the great Jelly Roll with J. in that cathedral in the Crescent City. We played our way of rhythms and melodies but kept the intent of grooving together. They worked on the ending, trying to get it off the beat. Ellis showed up while they were working. They didn't stop playing and he wouldn't have expected them to. Delfeayo was still waiting for some more microphone cable, which they'd had to send out for.

It never came while Wynton was still there. They would have to try to record again, in New York probably.

"I'm sorry bruh."

"Later."

"Later."

Ellis didn't get upset either. That's the way he was. He could come home when you were little and if you told him you just busted a window with a baseball the first thing he would say is, "Uh-huh." Of course then he would talk about it with you, you could be sure of that. My daddy liked to talk. In long sentences. But he would listen too. Stand there and listen to us tell all kinds of self-aggrandizing lies.

He could get mad, too, if you disrespected someone. And if I was playing with him and I didn't try to play music, but just showboated, he'd look at me very intensely and without the slightest drop of kindness. He did not condescend to us. You wanted to play some music, or you didn't. If you didn't want to play, you didn't get a pat on the back for being up there.

"Son," he would say if you were bullshitting. "What are you doing?" But he would say it as if he expected a profound answer. And since there was nothing of value in what you were trying to do, you just answered yourself. "I am bullshitting."

He wouldn't holler. He'd go on playing the tune himself.

It was my mama who did most of the punishing. Six boys and no girls. She kept us in line and did a lot of the dirty work. Took us to music lessons, to the doctor when we were sick, went to school when we showed our ass the wrong way. She made the most nutritious food for us and kept us from killing each other.

Once I got to eighth grade, I was practicing my horn at least four hours, sometimes six, every day. My father told me, if you want to be good and separate yourself from other musicians you have to be willing to do what they don't want to do. A lot might practice one or so hours, but almost none four or five. The trumpet is an unforgiving instrument. Cold metal on skin and lips, straining muscle pressed against teeth. You have to want to play it and keep on wanting it. You won't ever master it, only work with it and try to make it an extension of itself. Years of playing and studying and teaching, still the trumpet will reveal new truths. The jazz trumpet? All that bending, shaking, sliding, attacking, swooping, trying to make the metal sound like a human voice? That's not a joke.

Wynton had to run for it outside. He could tell it was about to rain again. He felt a little bad for J., who had come all the way down to make this recording and another one he was working on. A Christmas album. But he and Wynton would get it done. *Delfeayo should have been ready for us with those cables, or whatever it was that hadn't come. Why was it that something like that always seemed to happen?*

When I realized, growing up, that I wasn't going to be a professional baseball player because I wasn't even playing on my high school team, and I wasn't going to be a professional basketball player because I wasn't, I thought maybe I'd like to become a chemist or a biologist. I liked microscopes, and the fact of another entirely invisible world of action. The idea of mixing things, doing all those experiments, analyzing your re-sults, that also appealed to me. There was an order to it. A form. And if you were dedicated there were new worlds to discover.

So I studied hard, practiced hard. All the time in our house I'd hear music. My daddy practicing. And his friends would come by and I heard them. Idealistic men who wanted to swing even though virtually no one wanted to hear them. Alvin Batiste, Nat Perrilliat, James Black. Men who struggled and struggled but were dedicated. That's what I loved in them—they believed.

One day in junior high a friend of mine said I ought to try out for the civic orchestra.

"Okay. But I want someone to go with me. You come, too."

So we went down to where they were rehearsing and I saw the weatherman from TV playing timpani and all types of music teachers and adults playing in this amateur orchestra. We began playing Beethoven's Fifth and it was a sound that I'd never heard before. We were not even a mediocre orchestra but that music just got into your soul. An orchestra of fifty or so people in the Jewish Community Center leaving their everyday lives behind to play classical music each Monday night. It was worth missing Monday night football.

Two years before that, when I was twelve years old, I listened to one of my father's Coltrane recordings. The name of the record was Giant Steps. *I discovered that Coltrane had played with Miles Davis, and so had Wynton Kelly. The power of Coltrane's sound! I had the same experience with Beethoven. The power of Beethoven and Coltrane stunned me. I would go home from my orchestra rehearsals shaking my head. I would try to turn my friends on, but it was too late. The Chamber of Commerce had them. Our culture led you to believe that Beethoven was some white man's music and didn't say anything about Trane. That was the beginning of me understanding how up could be down. You had to really think about what you thought you knew.*

Branford and I started learning Bach chorales in class. We'd sing the harmony. Sometimes our high school jazz combo would sing the four parts of these chorales, soprano, tenor, alto, and bass.

When Wynton and Branford were singing Bach, they were also playing in their band, the Creators. They would have a gig, playing funk stuff, and had a good time playing it, got paid for it, too. And then at school they would sing the Bach harmonies. And listen to Coltrane and Miles and Blue Mitchell and Clifford Brown. Clark Terry and Freddie Hubbard. And Wynton was beginning to think maybe he wouldn't be a chemist or a ballplayer. Maybe he'd go to a music conservatory, follow in his father's footsteps and teach, because no one made much money playing—sometimes Wynton and Branford made more for a gig than Ellis. One summer Wynton went to a music camp in North Carolina. Then in his senior year he flew to New York City to try out for Juilliard. And after his audition, trying to find his way back to the apartment where he was staying, he happened to notice a sign that announced auditions for the summer school in the Berkshires at Tanglewood, run by the Boston Symphony Orchestra. Wynton had missed a Tanglewood audition in New Orleans because there was so much rain that day that the judge went home before Wynton arrived— soaking wet, having caught three buses and walked several blocks. So, now, here was a second chance. He went inside and introduced himself.

"You're seventeen. You have to be eighteen to apply for the fellowship orchestra," someone said.

"That's okay," said Gunther Schuller, the director of the school then. "He's here. Let's at least let him try."

The city of New Orleans was like a woman that you had to go to. You couldn't wait for it, for her, to come to you.

The trumpet, too.

Sweets Edison, the first time he heard me play, said, "Son, you got to get some weight in that tone."

You got to get it. It doesn't just come because you want it.

On another visit to New Orleans, the band was playing a gig at Tulane University, not far from Wynton's parents' house. But his parents weren't coming. It would be embarrassing if they made a fuss. Wynton's mother needed to take care of Mboya. And Ellis was away so much now, doing his own tours and playing with J., that he didn't need to come over and listen to his son the one night he was home.

The band had been off for a few days. Veal, visiting his parents, went to Pleasant Zion Missionary Baptist Church where his sister Deborah sang in the choir.

His parents had dinner for him and some of the cats after church at his house. Gumbo, whole crab claws in it. Two different kinds of sausage with the barbecue ribs. Then the men watched the New Orleans Saints play football on television.

Later, at the Tulane gig, Veal got out his bass and embraced it, played a few notes with his bow, and smiled.

"Sometimes you don't play and it is so nice to find you still have what you had the last time," he said.

Because the band was back where Veal grew up, some of his old friends had been calling him. But he hadn't told many of them he was in town.

"Most of my old friends were girls and I cut that out when I got married," he said.

Veal was married to a beautiful woman named Kim, who worked for Delta Airlines. It was a job she sought, so when she had a day off she could fly to wherever the band was and be with her husband. Veal was like a little kid on those days, waiting for her to come.

"Going to be with my baby tonight!"

Sometimes Kim would have two days off and she would travel with the band on the bus. There she'd be for a time. And then, at the next town, she'd have to fly out to get back to work. When everyone got on the bus the next morning she would be gone. Veal would be lost in daydreams. He'd stare out the window for a while, not quite hearing what anyone was saying to him as he made another triple-decker peanut butter and jelly sandwich. He ate so much peanut butter, he said, because of the braces on his teeth. He complained a lot about those braces, not mean-spirited complaints, but statements of fact. "My mouth hurts." He was a direct person. If he didn't like a hotel the band was in he always told Matt or Lolis, whoever was in charge. And he'd make suggestions to them about the schedule, because he got free air travel, too, being married to Kim, and he would be looking for a day off when he could fly and see his baby.

What was it like to have that feeling? To need to be with someone so badly you'd fly a thousand miles for dinner.

Swing Doom.

The band had a short rehearsal before the Tulane gig. This was a true homecoming for Herlin, too, and his wife Pat was there, driving their van. How happy Herlin was to see his children. His two boys, Herlin Jr. and Merlin, had been on the road with the band once. They went on the bus to Texas for a few days, their grandmother sending along fried chicken for the band. They each wore a suit to the gigs. At one of the gigs they sat on stage, behind a curtain near their father, and when the band played a second line they came out from behind the curtain and started dancing.

At Tulane, the band rehearsed a section of the Fagan ballet about skyscrapers.

"All right, Homey, you set up the groove," said Wynton. "And then those are like points of light in the tall buildings."

Outside students played touch football. It was fall but very warm. The wind rustled in the palm trees.

"This has got to be serene, this section," Wynton continued. "We got to establish a whole 'nother vibration from where we've been. We've been frantic."

Lolis Elie said there were many requests for passes. "But we haven't actually sold that many tickets," he lamented. He also reminded Wynton his father was away.

"E. is in Detroit," Lolis said.

Wynton had thought his father was at home.

On the way to the hotel to change after the rehearsal, Wynton stopped at his parents' house. And there was E. Was he in New Orleans or Detroit? Did anyone know what day it was?

Desi, Wess's wife, had driven down from Baton Rouge with Quad. They were coming with the band on the bus tomorrow, said Warm Daddy. Actually, they were coming with the band, but they were going in their own car. But Herlin's wife Pat was coming, on the bus, without the boys.

No one in the band formally coordinated these arrangements. They just happened. Pat was taking the week off from her office job. Desi, a beautician, must have cancelled all her appointments or not made any.

At the gig, the band played the skyscraper piece it had rehearsed.

"I had known about it for a year," Wynton confessed at the gig. "But I forgot they had to choreograph it. So when they called and asked, 'Where is the music?,' there wasn't any."

The audience seemed to think that was funny. Wynton never planned what he was going to say. Some nights he didn't say anything. Other nights he rambled at length.

Why wasn't there a bigger audience? This was where Wynton was from. The Crescent City. *That's why.*

standards & riffs

Herlin said you never think about the size of an audience, or the quality. You just were grateful you could play. And you never knew about an audience, he said. A noisy one, a quiet one, you couldn't know for certain who was hearing, who wasn't.

Each man sacrifices a lot to play this music. The amount of work is staggering, and almost all of it is away from home. When you have the chance to work and be with your family it actually feels strange, so I knew that Herlin was thinking about his family being at the concert tonight. About family life in general and the passing of time. The absence during important periods for loved ones. It's not easy, that part. Coming home and little things are different, the chair that was always in that corner has been moved to this corner. It sounds so silly but things like that get to you. And then, just when you're used to the routine, and they're used to you, you have to go again. Next time there would be some new story about something you missed, a part of family lore that did not include you. I knew that was a part of what Homey would be thinking. But he had too much dignity to joke about it. Too much pride. He was proud of what he and Pat did to provide for their family, but it came at a steep price.

Some nights I would be listening to the music but I couldn't help looking at Homey or Warm Daddy, Pine Cone, any one of the cats, they would be playing a solo, and I would think, "Damn! They're giving up a lot of their lives to be out here."

Most of them grew up in the church, but their spirituality represented more than that. It was something about the way we lived together, about the way everyone cared. What Veal called a spiritual vibe.

On the bus, when cats should have been tired, they were talking about music.

"Check this out, Cone. It's some King Oliver I've been learning."

"Sounds okay," says Cone.

We listened to an old recording of the tune.

"He's shaking it, boy. Shaking it a lot. And this one has that cry. Do you hear it?"

"Softer you play it, closer you're going to come to it," says Cone.

Veal put on some ballads, some Nat Cole. We had just played a gig, and we were driving all night to another one. We were all in the front of the bus, talking and listening to one another. Car lights punctuating the dark canvas of night. Cats missing their old ladies and families. Cone and Veal fixing sandwiches and some coffee for Harold. J. asking Cone to hook him up with a sandwich too. It was beautiful and it was lonely. Then, one by one, cats said, "T minus." And after a while went to sleep. But Cone stayed up with me, listening to King Oliver.

After the first set in New Orleans, after intermission, some of the people in the audience moved down closer to the stage. Even though there were empty seats the hall didn't feel quite so empty. There was some intimacy.

Wynton invited everyone in the audience who'd brought his instrument with him to come up on stage. Quite a few musicians did, including those who had attended a workshop earlier. Nicholas Payton came up. He was playing one of Wynton's old horns. Sometimes he reminded Wynton of Armstrong, the way he just set himself and blew. Wynton had attended Nicholas's high school graduation. He flew all the way from New York to New Orleans for it.

Now the band played "New Orleans Function" from *Majesty of the Blues*. Then came "Down Home With Homey," one of the tunes from *Soul Gestures in Southern Blue*. Wess's little boy Quad wandered on stage during that tune. Then the men played "Uptown Ruler," completing a New Orleans program of Wynton's music. One of the musicians taped the program. Listening afterwards, he said, "I can live with that."

Wynton was scared when he left New Orleans for his Juilliard tryout in New York. He knew what he could do on the trumpet. He'd been practicing. But he didn't know he would be okay until he started playing.

The first thing I played in the civic orchestra was Sibelius's Second Symphony and Ravel's Bolero.

At home, growing up, Wynton would hear his father talking with his friends. He'd be playing at a club somewhere and Wynton would tag along. It meant another night out of the house, and the next morning his father had to get up early and teach. But he never turned down work.

"Always take the gig," he said.

My mama didn't stand for any of that "I'm street"–type bullshit. You weren't going to kill her later with the dumb things you did. She would kill you now.

There isn't anyone in the world I could talk to quite the way I talk to my mother. But I might go home and hardly say a word to her. I took Skain with me and most of the time she watched him while I was working. And he slept at my parents' house while I stayed at the hotel.

Rob Gibson, Jazz at Lincoln Center's first administrative head, called Wynton in New Orleans and told him he was late with the copy for a program. The printer was waiting. It was going to cost $100 a day, goddamn it!, each day Wynton was late. Wynton told him he'd pay the $100.

D.J. Riley called Wynton too. Said he'd been sick for a while. Pneumonia. "I was with you spiritually, man," D.J. said.

The band was rehearsing King Oliver again. Joe Oliver was actually his name but he was called King. Louis Armstrong used to play in his band. At the end of King Oliver's life, when he was working as a custodian, Armstrong was playing in the town where King Oliver lived, and when he saw his old boss on the street he gave him money.

While the men rehearsed they listened to some of Oliver's original recordings. The recordings were scratchy and hissy but you could certainly hear the swing, delicate and hard driving. During the rehearsal, Skain sat a few rows of chairs behind his father, making paper airplanes with one of the men who wasn't playing. He was getting nudgy, Wynton could see it in his body. And the band had only been rehearsing a little while. It wasn't even lunchtime.

Little Skain got up and started running around the room. Wynton had to chase him and put him on his lap, and that's where he sat for the next tune. Wynton held him on his lap with one hand, his left, and with his right he held his cornet.

The room they were in was a trailer with a tin roof. It was an auxiliary classroom at Xavier University.

So Wynton played Oliver's "Snag It," with Skain on his lap, and suddenly on that tin roof you could hear the loud pelting of rain. Another New Orleans thunderstorm.

"Daddy," said Skain. "Daddy, I'm getting tired. I want to go home."

The musicians tried another tune. It was not the regular band. Homey was here, and Cone, but Cone was playing the bass. Nicholas Payton was going to be playing. And Dr. Michael White, who taught Spanish at Xavier but also played clarinet. He was an excellent player, and he knew a great deal about the music.

"Okay, let's run it down one more time and the next song," said Wynton.

He only had his own part in front of him, so when he asked one of the men to play the end of Oliver's "Chimes" Wynton had to read it from the score in his head.

"We got to remember not to play louder," he continued. "Let the intensity come out of the rhythm, not the volume."

Skain found some paper to draw on. Just then the electricity went off, because of the thunderstorm. Homey got up and danced. There was nothing to do but finish up that song and break for lunch.

A film crew was here in New Orleans making a documentary about Wynton. They were filming an interview with E. at the family's house. Dolores Marsalis wasn't happy that, once again, her house was turned inside out, upside down. Wynton didn't feel like dealing with the film either, but the crew had come all the way from New York and had a job to do. So after lunch with Dr. Michael White, Wynton talked to the director in the street outside his parents' house. Then he returned to his hotel to do his own work.

The next day it was time to return to New York. My mother stood in the doorway and watched us walk to the car that was waiting for us. I had my laundry, too, which she had done for me while I was home. She used to cook for me when I was home but she didn't that time.

Farid Barron, who was playing piano with us, was staying in my hotel suite so he could use the piano in it. He was there when I went to get my bags. He was wearing his Yankees cap and he was listening to CDs of our music. He was from Philadelphia. His parents thought he should be in school. He had a scholarship to Drexel, to study engineering. But he'd left that and left his parents and now he was up there in that suite, by himself, listening to Majesty of the Blues.

Farid. Such a unique character he already had a nickname. We called him Freeze, or the Frozen One.

A few days later, the band was in Shreveport, Louisiana. It was a fall day that felt like summer. Rob had arranged for a soundcheck, but Wynton told the cats to take it without him. He walked back to the hotel, which was just some bricks and glass over a bridge, near another interstate. A river ran through that city, a couple of blocks from the hotel. There was a bar or two there. Most of the old places were closed. A man stopped Wynton as he was walking by.

"Where you from?"

"Crescent City."

"Crescent City, yeah."

Crescent City.

2. Grace

Wynton was scribbling on his bed at the hotel. The night before, the band had played two sets in the ruins of Roman baths, up a hill past the Muse Mates, overlooking Nice, with the lights of that ancient city spread out below them like proverbial jewels. He'd had a little cognac, and he was just trying different things, and suddenly there was something that would work. Two months before it was due, he had finally started a piece, *Six Syncopated Movements*, he'd been commissioned to write for the New York City Ballet.

They had been in the country only a few days. They had just come to Nice from Bayonne, France. Walking around in that town, Wynton had seen a statue of Louis Armstrong outside a store. The shop owner had placed a Confederate flag in one of Armstrong's hands. About a block further Wynton had bumped into Lolis Elie and told him what he'd seen. Elie's French is a lot better than Wynton's, and they returned to the store to express their feelings.

"This is a free country," the shop owner said. And then he stormed outside to bring the statue in for the night. "We were just closing," he announced.

Before the gig that night in Bayonne, Wynton hadn't been able to find his shirts so Lolis loaned him one, but Wynton couldn't button the top button. He took his time.

"Life is long," he told kids at workshops. "Take your time."

But he still couldn't get the shirt to button. It was too small. So he left it open, with the tie loose, and on the way downstairs to the gig sang, "I'm so happy, I'm so happy."

Nobody noticed the shirt's missing button. The people in the audience must have thought Wynton loosened it because it was so hot. The band played a long time, and when Homey and Wynton did "Buddy Bolden" for an encore the people cheered so loudly it seemed you could have heard them from the next town, just as Buddy Bolden could be heard in Algiers across the river from New Orleans.

And then in the hotel bar we played until the bus left early in the morning, and some of the people who were still in the bar came outside to wave us farewell.

Nice was a beautiful place, a wonderful place. Bustling with a feeling of self-importance. Matisse lived in Nice so the whole city was a historic landmark. Just his name evokes a feeling for all that is lyrical and graceful and French.

There was a photograph in Wynton's trumpet case, of a boy from Norway, older than his sons, he must have been eleven or twelve. He was on his way to a band rehearsal and he was wearing a blue uniform. Blond hair. *He was proud to be a trumpeter, proud to be in a band. I bet he played the hell out of his horn.* He'd sent the picture to Wynton in the mail, and Wynton had carried it since, all the time he'd been on the road the last few months. It was with him when he finished *In This House, On This Morning,* which the band was playing now, or playing part of it. The whole two-hour piece was too long to play at a gig. Wynton had written it on the road, in Virginia when it was snowing; and in Atlanta while looking out a hotel window; and in Jackson, Mississippi; and the band learned it during a hectic, happy gig in Boston, where everyone stayed near Harvard and played at the Regattabar. That was a great gig, and now the band was playing sections of it in Nice. Last night, however, the band had played the whole first movement of *Griot.* That was a lot of music for some of the people who crowded into that amphitheater, and several left. Pianist Bobby Short had stayed. He'd heard something, he and his wife Gloria said to Wynton afterwards. He wanted to tell Eric Reed, who has been playing the piano in place of Marcus Roberts.

Eric Reed can hear, too, in long spans of time. He can process what everyone else on the bandstand is doing and not lose track of where he is. You've got to when you're playing jazz. Because things are changing too fast for you to process the changes otherwise. He plays with a deep understanding for the nuances of every musical situation. He can hear all the parts, even the tenor, which is the hardest to hear.

There is a prayer in the piece. I wrote some words, which took a long time to write:

PRAYER
To Thee, O Lord, We Say Yes, this day
And in this house, Yes swells in our souls
To praise Thy vast creation, and ring the bells whose melody
Affirms.
Oh! Yes!

Bells which sing of sweet love, Rebellion lost.
And though ten-thousand suns-rise.
Those bells yet ring still true.

Three yesses. Yes. Yes. Yes. Those yesses can get you in any-
where, from the lofty and pearly gates to the smoldering red-
hot gates down below.

Everybody on the bus had tried to help Wynton while he
was writing the text, everyone except Harold. But he might
have helped. *You never know where the next help in your*
world is going to come from. It could be something you re-
member, like the sunlight on our street in Breaux Bridge,
Louisiana, or an exquisitely dangerous woman you just met.
Once in Massachusetts Wynton's friend André Willis and
he were playing ball in the hotel's parking lot. It was after
midnight. The men couldn't see very well. André was a
minister at a church in Cambridge then, and he used to
come to all Wynton's gigs whenever they were near enough
for him to drive. That night André's wife stayed with her
parents, who lived near the hotel, while André and Wynton
played ball after the gig. *André is calm and warm, except*
on the basketball court. He has a strong game and hates to
lose.

Afterwards, as the two friends were walking to André's car
to drive to get some drinks and then pick up André's wife,
they passed a bush on the side of the parking lot. There was a
bird in it, singing.

Wynton sang the same pitch.

Pause.

The bird responded.

Wynton sang again, getting closer to the bush.

Soon that bird and Wynton were singing in a duet.

In France the band was also playing Todd Williams's piece, *Jubilee Suite,* which it had recorded with *Blue Interlude.* The end of the piece was called "Grace," which Wynton would describe on the bandstand as "the gift of day to day to which we all return after a period of strife or challenge or tension." *Grace is the knowledge that it is never too late to start or begin again, no matter what, while you are in this world.*

Wynton had written some of *In This House, On This Morning,* in a Boulder, Colorado, hotel bar, because there was no piano in his room, and the bar was empty.

As it was here, late on a summer's afternoon on the Mediterranean. The cats were coming into the lounge, unpacking their instruments. Swing Doom and Pine Cone had been windskiing—standing on waterskis with a kind of open parachute on their back, and when the boat that was pulling them went fast enough becoming airborne. Rob was looking for them right now, because the band had a rehearsal. Homey set up his drums. He hadn't wanted to participate in an extra gig; he and Wynton had played after the band arrived here, in a little town by the sea where you could look up from the stage and see the backs of the oldest houses on top of the hill above you. Homey would have liked that day off, but he didn't say so. When they returned home the band would go back in the studio to record, which meant Homey wouldn't have seen his family for almost two months. But he didn't say that.

Where is Veal? Why can't Rob find him? The part of the piece that the band was going to rehearse began with him, a long solo, then Eric came in, then Wynton, then Wess and Todd.

From the back wall, across the empty tables in the lounge in this very comfortable hotel, you could see out the big plate glass windows to the blue water. The palm trees were reminiscent of New Orleans. Cars rushed by. On the beach, hardly any of the women wore tops to their bathing suits, but you couldn't see that from here. But you could see a line of flags, of different colors, along the busy road, the flags blowing in the stiff, hot Mediterranean breeze.

Stiff. Hot.

Lord have mercy.

Now, at last, here was Swing Doom. Wynton knew that Veal was upset having to play like this without time to get ready, to take a shower and put on his nice potions and everything.

"Cone's coming, bruh," says Veal.

Jazz.

So the musicians begin again, a group of people trying to work something out.

Grace.

3. Massa's in the Cold, Cold Ground

Only two trains stopped each day in Montgomery, down the line from where the locomotives and coaches used to pull into historic Union Station. A single Pullman from the Louisville & Nashville REA Express, faded blue and rusted underneath, hid in the weeds at the far end of the station, the tracks on which it traveled paved over after its last run …

> *Where's my* Jubilo *notebook?*
> *Got to make more changes tonight*
> *About Ol' Mass.*

… The station's giant train shed, several hundred yards long, formed an elaborate parking lot for the offices, restaurant, and museum that now occupied a part of the brick and stone station, while Amtrak sold tickets for the northbound and southbound in a converted sugar-cane elevator, hard by the steep banks of the big bend in the Alabama River called High Red Bluff, or Hostile Bluff, or Thirteen-mile Bluff ...

When's this train pulling in?
Put my suitcase in the front of the car,
By the door,
Ain't nobody else on the train to steal it;
Put my Stetson overhead.
Get a little work done.
Hope this train goes faster than that motorcade.

... Nearly 300 years ago, a tribe of Alabama Indians was said to have attacked a small band of the first French explorers, killing three and critically wounding two. By the next century the site, recalled later as "the key to the Southeast," had become a famous wharf, where the spoils of the region's slave system, cotton, were shipped downriver to Mobile ...

"Clear the room."
So we cleared,
Leaving all them barbecued shrimp
Just waiting to be eaten.
And the Vice President's family came in.
I played "John Brown's Body,"
"The Battle Hymn of the Republic."

... and from there across the Atlantic to English mills. No outer trace of those horrors remained today. Instead, the river trees laced with green and the air slightly fragrant in the late winter Alabama afternoon, a couple on a date strolled past a paddle boat that took tourists for river rides along the fast flowing water in season, under the nearby bridge of an interstate highway...

> *Wonder if Clark Terry was there,*
> *Seeing him the other night*
> *Made that gig worth it.*
> *Remember the duet with Yo-Yo,*
> *He put some serious dick on that cello,*
> *He is a man who is a master;*
> *Went to a class he taught;*
> *I was 15, he was a boy then, too.*

... Whoever believed in ghosts would find them if he walked up from the station and wharf, up wide Commerce Street with its beautiful Victorian façades, past empty warehouses and boarded-up stores, to the corner of Dexter and Hull ...

> *Then the motorcade to the arena,*
> *Every exit we passed blocked off by police,*
> *Helicopter flew overhead,*
> *Still took forty minutes;*
> *President not there.*
> *Here's my notebook.*

... There, in the Dexter Avenue Baptist Church, the eloquence and power of the Reverend Martin Luther King Jr.'s first sermons once filled the sanctuary on Sunday mornings. Nowadays, the building had the feeling of being the oldest person at a gathering. Dr. King's first church stood only a block below the state capitol where Governor George Wallace ...

Driver: check all facts,
Beware of the lie
To hide the lie;
Watch out for cold words, because
All of everybody is never anything.
Reporters never let the truth get in the way
Of a good story.
People who are late, who are murdered
Who fuck up, who fuck:
We'll use it to sell trucks or razor blades or beer. Or
  music.
But don't ever get caught.
Papers love that,
Call it a great touching story,
And the righteous swoon, "How many? How
  much? When? With whom?"
Then cast stones.
Ol' Massa's in the cold, cold ground.

... once preached his doctrine of segregation and bigotry. Dr. King has been gone for more than a quarter of a century, and Governor Wallace, crippled by a would-be assassin's bullet in the 1972 presidential campaign, was dead, too. The center of the city, scene of pivotal Civil Rights battles more than a generation before, was depicted in murals on the walls of the basement of the church ...

Through deserted downtown streets
To station.
Which way is Blues Alley?
Many a night
Packed with folks.

Where's Harold Russell?
The little pit bull from Tennessee.
And we told him
Massa's in the cold, cold ground.

… They illustrated a story much of the present population of Montgomery knows only secondhand. As if to symbolize that change, a large portion of the populace had moved outward from the city's center …

The microphones kept feeding back.
Toon Yab Scab,
A hammer in his hand.
Driving over, told the driver to stop,
He went right by, under the railroad bridge,
Graffiti in big flowing letters:
"One Yal Hit My Boy On He Hade."
And we told him,
Massa's in the cold, cold ground.

… Shopping malls stood on farmland where plantation slaves used to bale cotton. Commerce Street quieted quickly after five on weekdays, but not everyone headed home from work. Downtown, inside a renovated movie palace where a jazz band was rehearsing, another son of the South played several bars of a Gershwin song…

Too tired to work
Too bumpy to write
Train finally moving
Capitol building lit up like a motherfucker
Nothing to do but wait

Like that time in Wilmington
Across the street from the opera house
Hard rain after soundcheck
Couldn't do nothing but watch
The rain.
Clifford Brown.
"Clifford Brown With Strings."
26 when he died;
Brownie.

… written when Montgomery's Union Station was thriving and Negroes who lived in Montgomery had to ride in the back of the city's buses and sit in a separate section of the theater. The song was "Embraceable You."

On the mall, under that tent,
How did Veal keep that bass
Warm enough to play?
And we told him
A bass will crack on you.
Homey doing his drumstick toss and twirl,
And we told him
You've got to keep those drums singing on the
    wind.
Massa's in the cold, cold ground.

4. The Deacon

Todd had left the band again. Todd Williams. The Deacon.

He and Wynton talked. Todd said he missed his wife. He wasn't happy being away so much. And he didn't approve of the way everyone lived. He'd become very religious, disapproved of the men's cursing, and never talked about other women.

"You can't expect everyone to believe like you, man," said Wynton. But Todd didn't seem to be listening.

They talked a long time, but they didn't settle anything, so a few weeks later, when Todd told Wynton about his decision to leave the band, it was a surprise. Inside of that surprise was the sense of some deep chasm. Wynton would have to find someone to replace Todd in the band; he knew that.

But who was going to replace Todd in his life?

The Deacon.

Who was always going to be working on his music, always showing up for the gig on time, always *there*?

The band closed the dressing room door after the next gig and that's when Todd told the rest of the men. They could hear people knocking on the door during their meeting, but they felt this was too important to interrupt.

The band always had meetings when something serious happened, like one of the men getting married. After Cone became a father the musicians had a meeting that was like a service. Wycliffe was there when the baby was born and then he returned that night to be with the band so he wouldn't miss a performance.

At the meeting about Todd, Todd spoke first. He talked about being in the band, what it meant to him, why he had made his decision.

"I'm going to miss you all," he said. "More than I can say."

Then the rest of the men spoke. Everyone said you have to do what you have to do. After each time one of the men spoke, he and Todd embraced. There was not a man in that room who did not understand what Todd was saying.

When Rob hugged Todd there was silence. By then maybe everything had been said that could be said. Whatever the reason, the silence was eerie. It made the men shudder.

And then Wess spoke, Wess who had played next to Todd all those nights. Wess began crying, and then Todd cried, and soon everyone in the room was wiping away tears.

Herb Harris took Todd's place for a while. Triple H., the men called him, because those were his initials. Or Burger King because that was his favorite food. The band was in Paris and the first thing Herb said when they drove through the city was, "Look, a Burger King!" And that's where he ate. Triple H.

After Paris we traveled to Amsterdam. You can find or get whatever you want or need, or think you want or need, in Amsterdam. Land of the tall people and canals. The Dutch love jazz music and having a good time. Of course you can be lonely here too if you want to be.

And then we stayed on the road in Europe for another four weeks. We were gone an entire month. Switzerland. Scotland. Germany.

We must have played at least twenty gigs. With a bus driver named Morris. Big old affable Englishman who used to be in the French foreign legion. Never even heard the name jazz. But ended up being a fan for life.

Twenty gigs all over Europe. Each place with a different language, set of customs, and relationship to jazz music and black folks. "Are you a team or something?" "It must be great to be treated like real artists here instead of discriminated against in America." "Why don't you rap?" Europeans think about jazz, America, black Americans, in interesting ways. Many times their view is tainted by the American press. You realize how racist the American media is when you go to places that don't have a black American population to provide an alternative re-

ality to the prevalent stereotype. When you have to deal with what people think of you based on the images they've seen, it can be quite painful.

At the end of the twenty cities we played at the great festival of jazz in Marciac. We come here every year. It's like coming home. How to explain a relationship that you develop with a whole city? Why? For some reason they adopt you and you love them. It happens. I sponsored a class of young musicians in Marciac when they were ten or eleven years old. Now they're all in their late teens and early twenties, but I still see some of them every year, and also teach new ones. The older ones come to a class and help out. Jean-Louis Guilhaumon is the president of the jazz festival, the mayor of the town, the dean of the middle school. He maintains integrity in an era of increasing difficulty. When the great tenor saxophonist Guy Lafitte was alive, he and bass king Pierre Boussaguet and I would go around to clubs and restaurants in the town and play all night. A girlfriend I had in Marciac told me that Guy came to her elementary school when she was a little girl. He was humor and soul and all that is great about jazz. Pierre and I miss him something terrible. We don't dwell on it too much. But we feel it and know it. We wear the berets of the wine makers and drink Armagnac and eat foie gras. Then we play music, music, music.

Once again I was late writing a piece, so every night I wrote music in my room after the gig. I wrote music on the bus, every spare minute, music. And then the next day I'd fax the music to New York. It was going to be cool.

As soon as we got back to the States, exactly five weeks to the day before the premiere, we recorded the music. But when we started to record there was something terribly wrong. The parts were full of mistakes. There were so many mistakes I told the cats to go home for a few days and we'd do the next section *on the road, wherever we were. We'd get space in a hotel to re-hearse and Rob would record it.*

And that is exactly what we did.

We had gigs to play out west and all around the Midwest. And master classes.

I hadn't seen my boys hardly at all, we'd been away all that time and now we were leaving again.

There were radio shows to do.

When was I going to learn the music for my upcoming classical recording? Learn it so I knew it.

And there was another commission to write, maybe even longer than this one, and I hadn't written a note.

Plus the apartment was a mess. The books were still in boxes. The records were stacked on the floor in my bedroom. There was no food in the refrigerator, except four loaves of raisin bread and some bottles of raspberry spritzer.

There was a Christmas show that was going to be taped. There were tapes of another recording to approve. And tapes from the Vanguard. I had to listen and make notations for Steve.

When Candace brought our two boys to my apartment, she looked around and shook her head. "You've got to do better than this," she said. "It's like the room of a college student who just left home. When are you going to stop living like this?" She said now there were three children in the house.

Another Goodbye

Before Wynton left New York on the next tour it was summer weather again for a day, and he walked to get the boys for a last night before he left.

He had not packed. Actually, he had not unpacked. Now it was time to pack again.

He walked from midtown to where he used to live. It was about a thirty-block walk and took about an hour.

The air had its New York smell, the exhaust and the dirt on the street and the smell of people passing you and the pretzels at the corners. But there was also the smell of summer; it was fall, but you could fool yourself that day.

Wynton walked past the place where he used to play basketball when he lived downtown.

"What' say, bruh!"

"Watch out!"

"Inside, inside!"

At the corner a man stared at Wynton and nodded. But he didn't ask Wynton for anything. Wynton nodded back and walked on.

In his head he sang the melody for "Buddy Bolden," just Wynton playing, Wynton and Homey.

Another Tour

Flying west, Wynton worked with Ronnie Carbo on the corrections to one of the three pieces he was writing. Ronnie was from New Orleans although lately he'd been living in Boston. Another Berklee Conservatory graduate, he was married to a pediatrician. For a while he worked in the crew for New Kids on the Block. He had to leave that gig to serve in the Persian Gulf as a marine. He was in the front lines, in reconnaissance, across the border in Iraq, with people getting shot all around him and men so scared they were shitting in their pants. And that was something anyway, said Carbo, taking a shit in Iraq. You had to hop out of your bunker very fast and hope no one shot you before you hopped back in. Men saved any kind of paper they had to wipe themselves, because the marines didn't receive t.p. in their rations. When Carbo came back from the war he worked a little longer for the New Kids but he was getting tired of it. He was too good a musician. He played several instruments, and he could copy music. He was the only man Wynton knew who could take apart and put back together both an M-16 and a musical score. Ronnie had known Swing Doom in New Orleans. Once they were in a restaurant in New Orleans and the food was lousy so they just got up and left. But that was a mild episode for Carbo.

Car-bo!

Not quite Wynton's height, Ronnie has short hair and pointed ears with little earrings and he talks quickly in a voice that has many different pitches, so it almost seems like he's singing sometimes when in fact he is just talking. When Carbo flew west with the band he carried a briefcase made of metal that was filled with pencils and a pencil sharpener and all sorts of inks and erasers and whiteout fluids. These were his tools. First he'd flown down from Boston to New York and worked at Wynton's apartment for a few days. Wynton could tell him what to do and he just went ahead and got out his pencils and started doing it, for hours at a time. He slept even less than Wynton. And he never complained. For a week he corrected parts at Wynton's apartment and on the road and finally—the band was in St. Louis by then—Ronnie had enough corrected parts that the musicians could try again to rehearse the premiere and record it.

Rob arranged for a room to record at the hotel. The band had just had a twelve-hour bus ride, and the men had not yet unpacked. Lolis arranged for room service to be available in the room where the men rehearsed, which was actually one of the hotel's dining rooms.

I couldn't believe there was that much music. And that hard.

A waiter brought in some drinks and ice.

"They got drinks and ice for y'all."

It was two o'clock in the afternoon in St. Louis.

Right off, Wynton had to make additions in the parts for Homey and Veal. What he wrote for them was always more by the way of suggestion—a chord, a riff, a groove—and they would work with it.

Chandeliers lit the dining room. It was a odd feeling, rehearsing there with these chandeliers and thinking about the martinis that must have been consumed in that place, the cigarettes smoked, the meals eaten, the propositions made.

Lolis came into the room—the Mayfair Room, it was called—Lolis came in with a handful of sharpened pencils and passed them out to the men.

Occasionally someone else staying at the hotel would peek through the door. Later, bolder people walked right in, took a seat, and listened. It reminded the musicians of what would happen in a club.

Lolis left and came back with both a small towel and a washcloth for Veal to wipe down the finger board and strings of his bass. Veal chose the towel.

Veal was angry at Wynton because he had wanted to spend the evening with Kim because the band had no gig tonight. Now, instead of flying to Kim in Atlanta, he had to rehearse.

"Say, Rob, do you have stuff set up for tomorrow so we can record?"

Wynton loved asking Rob those kind of questions. Rob thought it was his job to do certain things without being asked and so it got under his skin when Wynton checked on him. *I just liked to mess with him, get his blood flowing right.*

"The reason we kept going over these two pages was that if we could get those two pages we could understand a lot of the piece," Wynton said.

The afternoon wore on.

"Okay, we've got to go over the transition," Wynton continued. "This has to have a majestic sound."

Just then High Point, who had been standing on a dining room chair to take a picture, fell off.

Miraculously, neither he nor any of the band's equipment—or his, for that matter—was hurt. And there was equipment all over the Mayfair Room. Triple H's tenor sax in its case on the floor. Wynton's mutes on a table near him. Music manuscript pages covering the next table. Ronnie's whiteout bottles and Scotch tape.

It was getting to be evening outside and the room began to darken.

Wynton corrected two hundred measures a night of this new piece. It would be done by the end of the week.

The musicians would record the next day. And there was a gig to play. The band stayed another day and recorded a little more and Wynton went in the afternoon with Wess and Cone to East St. Louis to Miles Davis's old school, Lincoln High. They heard the school band, which Wynton's friend Ron Carter directed. They listened to the kids in that school in the middle of a city that everyone else in the area seemed to pretend didn't exist, heard them play and told those kids how lucky they were to have Ron Carter giving them all his time and love. Wynton told them you've got to be a part of something that you find on your own. Ron Carter was helping them find it, he said.

And the kids asked questions. No, Wynton said, he never thought he was going to be popular. "I looked at my daddy and he was the greatest musician I knew and he wasn't famous."

The kids are so beautiful at Lincoln. They're fortunate to have teachers and parents to help them. Many kids in East St. Louis, and all over really, are caught in the crossfire of a cultural battle without a helmet, let alone a weapon. There's nowhere to go for cover. They just get slaughtered. Man.

We had more work to do. Every town we stopped at during the rest of that tour, we rehearsed. I corrected more of the score with Carbo. In Lafayette, Louisiana, where we stayed two days about a week after we left St. Louis, we rehearsed so late into the night that cats were sleeping on their chairs during breaks. Before we got to Lafayette we'd already been to three other states and ridden over a thousand miles. We were like those caravans in the days of the Old West, except there was only one bus in ours and it seemed like we went around in circles.

Riding back in the van to the hotel from the gig in Lafayette, Rob put on a tape of what we had just rehearsed.

"Rob, please shut that shit off. All I need to do is get my black ass in bed and sleep."

Then the tour was ending and there was no point in taping any more music. We would be in New York again in a few days.

I missed the Deacon.

I missed J., although he would be playing with us for the week we were in New York.

I missed my kids. All of the cats missed their loved ones.

We did a few workshops, too, and I met someone and invited her to the last gig on that tour. She didn't come on the bus with us but met us there. Met me. I was afraid she would get scared and stay home.

Soft, honey brown. Quiet voice. Sweet sweet sweet.

She was there after the gig that night, an autumn night in the South smelling of the summer, and we walked back to-

gether through the streets to the hotel. We were clowning and carrying on like people do when they're ēnamored about being enamored. I was carrying my horn on one arm, her on the other. The cats passed us on the bus, looking and laughing. And so were we.

Later, standing at the window of my room, I watched the late-night trucks that passed by the hotel, their headlights shining. It was warm enough to open the window. The breeze gave me goosebumps down my bare back, down my legs, all the way to my toes. How the union of opposites reveals the majesty of existence. Sad plus happy equals the blues. Intimacy plus danger equals sex. A thing as basic as breath equals in plus out. I thought of the unruly perfection of a man and a woman together.

One plus one equals one.

But if you forget what time it is,

One plus one can equal three. (Well, that's what Crouch says anyway.)

And of course there are always those who would have you pay

For having a good time

For loving a woman

For getting high or drunk

> *Or talking and laughing too loud*

> *Or cussing a motherfucker out*

> *Or just for being your beautiful sweet self. Hmm.*

You want to know what I was taught by all those jazz musicians I grew up around? There is no price to pay for life except to live it. And if somebody wants to make you pay a price for how you live, fuck em.

And with the blue-edged blade of love, him cut sharp both ways.

> *Sweet and the bitter.*

And when it cuts you to the bone
    And you can still make love as if the bite of that razor is
what opened your heart for the first time and set your blood
on fire
        and set your soul free
            And when every time you play is like that time

Then you gon' find jazz in the bittersweet blues of life.

four

Basketball before the gig. Good crowd, new hall. Emptied quickly afterwards.

Walked together.

—*My father lived near here.*

—*My father was a riverboat captain.*

Wispy blond hair, thin waist, full soft deep voice.

Took her hand as they walked.

Where to go?

—*Here's a place.*

—*What would you like?*

—*Coffee.*

—*Two coffees.*

Supposed to rain tomorrow. No rain that night. No rain and footsteps and a swinging lobby door.

the sound of laughter

The band was staying in Virginia. It was early spring, the grass still yellow and the trees just beginning to bud. After the Civil War, Robert E. Lee became president of a university, Washington and Lee, and the band was playing there. When the musicians arrived in Lexington, they discovered that the wife of the promoter had prepared a special meal for them: chicken and real mashed potatoes with homemade gravy and bread that must have taken her all day to bake.

But the men didn't eat it right away, after soundcheck. First, they went and played some ball.

The gig was in a building next to the train station, but now the tracks were gone and everything was fancied up with glitter and glass, especially in the rotunda. You could walk in from where the station used to be, next to a bridge that was still standing. It was eerie because you expected to hear a train whistle at any moment and feel the thunder of the train as it came in. Instead there was a box office for the theater. The box office was closed because the gig was sold out.

We'd only been in Virginia for a day. A chilly, gray day. We'd played a gig at another college the night before and they served us something that was supposed to be boeuf bourguignonne, that's what they actually called it, but you could tell it was made from some type of government beef.

Yes indeed.

And when one of the cats asked for bread the waitress said, "They didn't send any over."

Why is it when something goes wrong it's always "they"?

After that gig the musicians had still been hungry. Wynton and I went to a salad bar kind of place across the highway from the motel. A few college kids that he'd met at the gig came with him. They were sweet, talking about themselves. One of them was very religious. She was preaching the sermon the next morning at a church service on campus. *She was coming from the "Thou shalt not" frame of reference. You had to confess for having bad breath. But she knew she was beautiful. Everyone knew.*

We got to talking about race, and of course sex. Religious people love to talk about sex so that they can act horrified by what really attracts them. It's always difficult to speak on race, especially with people from different regions of the country and different generations. Many students I've met around the country like to relate everything about race to what they see in videos, or hear about. They think they're battling police brutality, or not being served quickly in a restaurant, two media favorites. Then a lot of these same students will kill themselves to sit at the Negro table in the cafeteria. The richness of Afro-American history is of very little importance to them, let alone the significance of an art form like jazz. Most students have never heard a single piece of jazz. And these are college students. And very intelligent young people.

These particular students were not like that. They were in-terested in what a jazz band did on the road. They wanted to understand why the black and white of things was still so diffi-cult. And some things just can't be simplified.

At a gig in Shreveport, Louisiana, a white limousine had picked up the band at the hotel and taken us to the downtown Strand Theater for a soundcheck. As the driver, a large, silent, middle-aged white fellow, turned a corner to bring the car to a stop by the marquee he had asked Wynton if this was the right door. "Oh, that would be the door for *him*," Wynton replied, indicating me, who happened to be sitting next to the driver. "You can let Moss off here. Then you can take the Negroes to the side door around back." The driver froze, staring at Wynton in the rearview mirror. He stopped the limo in front and waited. No one inside the car moved. Then from the rear seats laughter began, first as a high-pitched single cackle and then swelling to a chorus of howls. The driver shook his head and began laughing too.

Wynton asked the girls about their school subjects and their families and then one of them, the one who was giving the sermon, drove him back to the motel. Wynton had awak-ened that morning with a tune in his head and he was eager to write it down. He said thank you very much for the ride and worked alone in his motel room, except once he knocked on the wall because Wess was in the next room, and Wynton asked Wess to bring his sopranino so he could hear something he'd just written. Later, Wynton told a young woman from New York whom one of the men had met that she could ride on the bus with the band the next day and she said she had to ask her mother who was in the lobby down-stairs. Her mother said yes.

To play ball in the college gym at Washington and Lee Uni-versity, the men had to walk across an old trestle and find the gym among many buildings on a campus that looked like the Civil War in an old-fashioned film. *Thinking about General Robert E. Lee, playing ball near where he lived after the war, and then walking back to the place for the food, how the air smelled in the late afternoon of wetness with the leaves that hadn't all been raked in the fall. How it smelled the same way when the stench of panic and guts, horseshit and gunfire painted the air grey and black and the ground red and blue and gray as the treasonous forces of Lee waged war against these United States of America. Lee not only has a college, he even has a statue in the heart of New Orleans for his herculean efforts to destroy this country. Yee-hah. Somebody bring me a hot toddy.*

The ground was moist and a few flowers were trying to come out. Forsythia was in bloom. Across the way from the field, which looked out on the Shenandoah Valley, were the ruins of a building called Liberty Hall. *In my head I was hearing the tune I'd started writing the night before. It was a gospel tune.*

When the band drove back to the hotel to get dressed for the gig they passed the Stonewall Jackson Hospital, then a row of similarly-shaped houses. *And which house of the houses we were passing belonged to the woman who had cooked us food today? What was she doing now? Taking a shower maybe, before she got dressed for the gig, the hot water pouring all over her body, feeling good. And there must have been families in a lot of those houses, some of them eating dinner, and probably an old man lived in another house and an old woman a few houses down. Some people fighting and ruining each others' lives, others confiding in and consoling each other. That's how the world works, you meet people every day and you talk to them but you don't know what they have to go through, what their life is like, all these lives here, each infinitely different, yet all being lived right here right now, a thing never to be seen again.*

You don't necessarily learn about jazz in school. Many folks have this idea that jazz means you're up there on the bandstand playing whatever comes into your head, and hopefully when you're done the other cats will be about done, too. It isn't like that at all. Jazz improvisation is the creation of blues-based melodies in the context of harmonic, rhythmic, and timbral variation. There's a logic to its imposition of order on what would otherwise be chaos. And we all create the logic as we go along. The most important emotion in jazz is joy. But you don't create that joy just by feeling good. You create it by feeling terrible. Worse than that. About all the bullshit that has been put on people and continues to be heaped on. You have an empathy, a desire to improve things, to say stuff can be another way, not just about black people but the spiritual condition of all people. You've got to play. Together. You can't play jazz alone.

Jazz is also like the skyscrapers that even in Virginia I saw in my mind as we drove back to the hotel, dark now, cold, someone said it might snow, and I saw those skyscrapers in Manhattan in the snow and how they had this form, together, laid out in the grid of the Manhattan streets, but on each floor of just one of those tall buildings something different was happening. There was a stockbroker on one floor. A law office on another. Somewhere in that building someone was looking at the snow while they were making love. And others were explaining why they drove the company to bankruptcy.

The musicians got ready for the Virginia gig, Swing Doom taking the longest time with all his potions, everyone doing what Homey calls the five S's: sleep, shit, shave, shower, shampoo. Wynton didn't take a nap. He'd take his naps in the next life. There was a boxing match on the TV while he was getting dressed. Watching it reminded Wynton of the time he played the national anthem at the Holyfield-Douglas fight at the Mirage in Las Vegas. The owner of the Mirage had invited him.

The thing is, I don't really like to play the national anthem. Not because of any 1970s politics, but because I've messed it up a lot of times. I feel jinxed playing it. I can remember playing it at a high school basketball game in 1975 with an ad hoc group from the band. Everyone started falling out and messing up until the only player carrying on was a lone brave clarinet. David Vitter. All the opposing fans started laughing and hooting. We were embarrassed as hell. So I only agreed to play it because Veal has always loved Holyfield, and it was a way for him to see the fight. We walked out into the ring and played the anthem. Just trumpet and bass. I don't know how we sounded, but we were looking damn good. I had on a red jacket and Veal had his cutest tie on. After we played we dapped each other and sat ringside to watch the fight.

The ring was built behind the hotel, in one of the parking lots. Wynton felt the boxers looked lonely even with all those people around them. It wasn't like a gig Wynton played. *They were worried. Mess up on a gig, you go home mad. Mess up in a fight, you could lose your life.*

The only thing more defining than a behind-whipping is the love of your mother. I got into various scrapes when I was growing up, and in general didn't mind going into the physical arena, even though I was just a lil' ol' string bean. When you hand a butt-whipping out, it never crosses your mind, except when you brag and talk trash. But when somebody whips your ass, whew! You learn many things at once. First, you don't control when it stops. Second, other people have will and heart too. Third, it keeps on hurting long after it's over. After you've had your ass whipped, you never whip another person's butt with the same relish. That's why I always feel for boxers. Yeah, they're famous, and make a pile of money, but handing out or receiving a public boodie whipping is a rough way to make a living.

In Las Vegas the day after the Holyfield fight, the gambling tables in the casino were going at breakfast. Another friend of Wynton's works in Las Vegas, a friend Wynton knew when they were growing up. The friend came to see Wynton once when the band was playing Vegas. His name was Thedo. Thedo had lived across the street from Wynton in Kenner.

"Wimp," Thedo said to Wynton. Only his childhood friends called him Wimp.

"Wimp, we were *country*! Sitting in that little house of yours near the railroad track listening to Coltrane. 'My Favorite Things,' that's what we were listening to."

The two boys hopped a train once. It went about a mile. Wynton used to call Thedo Stevie because he liked Stevie Wonder. Thedo and Branford used to fight sometimes over marbles. Wynton didn't see Thedo after he left home but they'd talk on the phone. Wynton might be practicing the classic cornet solo, "Carnival of Venice," and he'd call and play it for Thedo on the phone.

People called him heavy, greasy, or just fat. He was always good-natured, but kids liked to mess with him, tease him all the time. The type of pure cruelty that is the specialty of children. One summer when we were nine or ten, he started swinging these nunchucks, a martial arts weapon that consists of two short sticks joined by a short metal chain. Every day he would walk around with these things and people would tease him. "Fat boy running around with them sticks in his hand. Look just like a big old pig." Well, after about a year, he became a virtuoso at swinging these nunchucks. That was the end of people fucking with him. And that was one of my first great lessons on the transforming power of patient persistent practice.

When he came to see me in my hotel room in Las Vegas it was like nothing had changed between us. He was playing piano in a group called Hot Stuff, at another Las Vegas hotel called the Flamingo. He drove me to our gig and then he came back after his and heard the end of our second set.

Thedo Lewis. His mama could make some good crawfish bisque too.

That was the Las Vegas trip when Harold Russell got stopped on the way for speeding. It happened as the band was coming through Utah.

Wynton had given Harold a video camera for Christmas and Harold was trying it out. He had it set up in the front of the bus, so when you watched the video you saw all the mountains the bus passed and a school bus full of children who made a motion with their fingers, scolding Harold as he passed them, because he was going so fast, probably around a hundred. Zap! The radar got him. You could see the cruiser coming up alongside in the video of where the rearview mirror on the bus was. Harold said later he was thinking to himself, "I'm cooked, this fine is going to cost at least three hundred dollars."

The trooper was young. He took Harold's license and registration.

"Who you carrying?" the trooper asked.

Harold told him. The trooper went back to his car for what seemed like the longest time.

"We're cooked," Harold said.

Finally the trooper came back. He said he loved jazz. And then the trooper said he had some of Wynton's records. He said he was going to give Harold a warning. No ticket. Just a warning.

"I could kiss that motherfucker's ass!" Harold said afterwards. And then he played the video for all the cats, because a lot of them were sleeping when it happened, and when it came to the part about the warning Harold said, "I *am* going to kiss his ass. If I ever see him again that's what I'm going to do."

Harold Russell.

It wasn't snowing yet but it was cold when the musicians came downstairs and outside for the ride from the hotel back to Washington and Lee University. High Point was a little late, which was unusual. Generally, he and Warm Daddy were the first ones down and they were waiting on Homey or Reginald or Pine Cone. Or they were waiting on Wynton.

We deal with it. It's like it is on the bandstand. You have to know how to interact with everyone. You have to deal with the situation, not with what you had in mind beforehand. You're constantly assessing the present.

Jazz.

Something about just the sound of the word I love.

JAZZ.

jazz.

A lot of great musicians hated the word. Max Roach. Duke Ellington. I understand where they are coming from, but that's a beautiful word. (jazz)

Waiting in the dressing room before the first set, the musicians played some blues. Wynton made up some words.

"Take them, take them," he sang, and then he made a little electric guitar sound with his voice before he continued singing.

Twang. Twang. With a nice fast vibrato on the end.

"Please baby, take them.

"Take them draws

"Please baby, take them draws, lawd.

"Take them draws on down."

Twang-twang.

Wynton stopped singing and picked up his horn. Wess and Veal were already playing. And Cone. Now they played a real blues, and they made the harmony as they played. Four-part improvised harmony. They kept playing that blues until it was time to go upstairs to play the gig. *Which is what jazz is about.*

We do it every night. We're out here together, on the road, learning to be men. It's not just being someone who can play, though what we play is hard. I know a lot of good musicians who couldn't play what the cats in the band play.

But it's got to be more than that. It's like what you know about your old lady without you saying it or her either. It's just something you both know, inside, something very important about living in the world.

Swing Doom says we're a band that will be remembered in history. I don't know about that. But his feeling that way means a lot to all the cats. It's part of our pride about being together. We don't have cliques, no "This is the rhythm section and this is the horns." Of course when we're playing there might be musical differences, but we work them out. Sometimes I have to be the leader and make decisions the brothers don't like. But I try to become more mature about dealing with cats as we go along. Jazz musicians will quit if they don't like their environment, especially when they know they can get other gigs.

Most of the cats grew up in a church tradition. When I first knew Swing Doom he was playing in a church group with his father. The group was called the Spiritual Commanders and Reginald played the electric bass. His daddy still has his group. They used to tour some, back when Reginald was with them, but mostly now they play in New Orleans, which is where Reginald's from. And Warm Daddy is actually from Brooklyn but he married a fine woman from Baton Rouge, Louisiana, and that's their home now, a couple of hours from New Orleans. He went to school in Baton Rouge, at Southern University, which is also where Swing Doom went to school. Why we call Reginald that, well, the first part is easy enough to understand if you've ever heard him play. But so is the second word, Doom, because not only does Reginald swing every time he plays but there is an incredible weight to his sound, a depth.

Doom.

Swing Doom. Ba-Doomski.

I love watching him play when we're on the bandstand. A lot of times he plays with his eyes closed. It's as though he's communing with the music, with the sound of each note. He possesses a great integrity and pride about his musicianship and about jazz music. This sings through his playing.

I watched him that night in Virginia, and across the stage from where I stood Homey looked at me and we held that contact. So much in a look like that. Homey with all his children back home, having to leave them each time to come out on the road, he's been doing that longer than any one of us, always swinging, driving the band, relaxed and warm. All the cats swinging the blues that spring night in Virginia and the chill in the air after, the ride back in the van to the motel, leaving early the next morning, leaving on another gray day with snow-flakes falling in the Blue Ridge in the Shenandoah Valley, chasing the swing, and Harold Russell shouting, "What the fuck! Let's go to Carolina!"

Deryle Sings the Blues

We've left the snow behind in Virginia. Into the bright bright sun! We'd be in Charlotte, North Carolina, by late morning.

Wynton reread a letter that had been placed in his trumpet case the previous night during the first set.

"Dear Wynton," it began. "We don't know each other and probably never will, but I feel I know you from listening to your music. You know what I mean."

No question mark.

"My boyfriend and I will be listening to you tonight. He doesn't know yet about your music, but I'm working on him. There's a song I was wondering if you'd play. Willie Nelson used to sing it but when you played it on a record I heard you didn't sing it. Do you ever sing? I can't remember the name of the song but you will know."

It was a Monday morning. Out the window the world was going to work in clear, crisp air.

Wynton had stayed up late working on a piece. *It takes forever to get started on it, then I get obsessed with it. When I get tired, I think about Victor Goines. He came out here with one day's notice to play the Deacon's book. Man, he wanted to be out here so bad, he would stay up all night practicing his horn in the back of the bus. It made all of us reassess our level of seriousness. Vic.* He wondered where in the audience the woman who wrote him that note had been sitting. He thought he could tell, looking.

Wynton was leading a workshop at an all-black college in Charlotte. This was the third workshop in three days. Wynton had awakened early that day for a meeting with Lolis. When he went to bed the night before around two-thirty, it was the earliest he'd gotten to bed in three days. He had been listening to another edit of a new recording, being released a few months later. And the band had driven out to a school for a basketball game, less than an hour after they'd arrived in Charlotte at seven-thirty.

After the Charlotte workshop, Wynton went to an art gallery to talk with the owner about Romare Bearden, a painter whose work Wynton loved. Then he walked across the street back to the site of the night's concert, an old church turned into a hall, and he was actually a few minutes early, something that rarely happened.

In came a television crew to do a quick interview for the evening newscast. The rest of the musicians arrived as the interview started, and soon they were playing a blues while the TV crew shot some more footage. Music stands had just been brought in, so Wynton could call a rehearsal. When the rehearsal ended, some of the musicians went back to the gallery. Wynton still had to eat and get dressed.

It happens too fast. And there is no free time. Elvin Jones once told me, "It was all over so fast," about the time he spent in the John Coltrane quartet.

In Charlotte we were staying in a brand-new hotel, but over the weekend we stayed in a hotel right on an interstate highway. One bad hotel doesn't make that much difference, but when you're doing one-nighters, a string of sad hotels can really hurt your feelings.

The band had had to hire a driver for basketball that night in Charlotte. The trip was about ten miles and the driver wanted $40 each way to take them. And she wanted to be paid in advance for both trips. The men had to trust her to come and pick them up when they were finished playing. They gave her a time and when that time came they went outside to wait for her and there was no van.

"I knew it," one of the cats said. "We should have asked Harold to drive us."

But Harold was asleep. Whenever the band came into a new town, after the band's stuff was off the bus and the drums and other equipment had been taken to the gig, Harold was on his own until it was time to pack and move on. Once in a while he might put on his Sunday finest and come to the gig, maybe if his wife Darlene was along, but usually he stayed to himself, watching TV or a movie, doing his laundry. And cleaning the bus. Harold ran a clean bus. He vacuumed it and washed the bathroom and restocked the refrigerator at every stop. *Harold Russell. Numero Uno.*

Harold couldn't help the band get back to the hotel after that basketball game. *We'd have never woken him; we've only done that once when there was nothing else we could do, and we were sorry. Not because Harold complained. He never complains, not counting that time in Pittsburgh when we got to the hotel, downtown, and the parking space that was supposed to have been saved had been taken and the hotel manager said no one called to reserve the space. You've never seen that type of heat come out of someone. A venomous outburst of pure profanity. Nouns, verbs, and adjectives. All vile.*

Everyone was supposed to meet the driver in the parking garage of the University of North Carolina at Charlotte campus, which is not really in Charlotte but in the outskirts. No one could phone the taxi company because the gym had been locked. No one had a cell phone with him.

It was one of those spring nights where the temperature is just in the chilly range, what you'd call cold if you lived in the north and summer had just ended, but in the spring seems almost balmy, with the smell in the air of things growing. It was a fairly clear night, so you could see the stars.

The men had brought their own basketballs, so they dribbled them on the pavement by the garage. Finally Wynton sat on his, which he had placed on the ground. He wanted to be back at the hotel, working on his music or maybe calling someone. He was tired.

I remember when I was in high school, my daddy was a teacher, he taught jazz at the New Orleans Center for the Creative Arts. He worked gigs at night until one, two, three in the morning. That was a hell of a grind. Trying to feed those six kids. But I never heard him complain. He always seemed to be thinking about something better. So, in a far more trivial way, it was the same sitting on that basketball waiting for that ride. I could complain. I could get deep into the crack of someone else's behind, whining about why this wasn't properly arranged so we don't have to waste our time. Or I could work on some music while I was sitting there, work on it in my head, I mean. Maybe a little of that spring air and the stars might sneak into my sound.

"Lolis! Where's that van, bruh?"

Lolis looked at Wynton and shrugged and frowned.

"I'm talking to you."

"Uh, boss, uh, I was . . . It'll be here real soon, boss. I promise."

"Shit! What are we paying you lazy darkies for anyways. I want that van here now or I want your ass looking for another one, you understand?"

Wynton couldn't keep the vibe. Lolis broke into loud laughter. The other men started clapping and singing one of their favorite refrains. "We done come a mighty long way, but we got a long way to go." Veal and Homey took the bass. You could hear their deep voices echoing in the cavern of the garage.

Smoking a cigarette with the ashes spilling all over the dashboard of the van, the driver arrived.

We'd been on the road for a long time.

We'd been all over the country. All over the world. We'd played for school kids in East St. Louis and black-tie crowds at Lincoln Center in New York City. And no matter where we were, the cats in the band came to work. That was something Art Blakey taught me.

"Son," he'd growl. "I always play the same. Always."

He meant that no matter where we were, with long drives between gigs, and no matter how tired he was, he tried to give a great performance. And he did. I never saw Art Blakey bull-shitting on a bandstand. Two hearing aids, no sleep, twenty-two hour car ride, hungry, lonely, after fifty-something years of gigs, tonight he swings his behind off.

"Music wipes away the dust of everyday life from your feet." Blakey used to say that all the time. "You never find an ar-mored car following a hearse." Blakey.

Before you get on the jazz bandstand, you have to ask your-self, Why am I playing jazz? What is the meaning of this?

In Chapel Hill, our next stop, we actually did two workshops, one at the high school and the other at the university. At the high school there was this little boy, four years old, he'd come because his father had arranged the workshop. I played with the school's jazz ensemble. We played some blues. And while we were playing, the boy, whose name was Deryle, came up onto the stage next to me and he started singing. Without training or directions or anything he sang the blues in perfect form. He was so young, it made me think of all the musicians I'd recruited for the band over the years.

He kept singing. Everyone in the place started clapping.

School had been out for about forty minutes, but a lot of the students stayed anyway. Asking question after question. Later that evening, Deryle's parents had a party for us at their house, a soulful affair with all types of good down-home vittles and lots of loud laughter. The next morning, Deryle rode on the bus with us to the restaurant where we stopped for breakfast. Made us late! Because Lolis, when he counted heads before we left the hotel parking lot, forgot he should be counting one ex-tra with Deryle on board, so when he got to eleven Lolis said to Harold, "Let's go." And it wasn't until we got to the restau-rant that we discovered we'd left Steven Scott, who was our pi-anist for those gigs, at the hotel. Lolis thought he was in his bunk on the bus, sleeping.

Back in Oakland

Wynton was sitting at the table in the front lounge, finishing his second bowl of Cocoa Krispies as the bus neared Oakland. The band had driven up from Fresno that morning, and even though it was around lunchtime half the men were asleep.

Rob stood near Harold, holding directions to the hotel.

"Say, bruh," Wynton said to Rob. "Who decided we should stay at the Marquis in Los Angeles?"

"Preferred, I guess," answered Rob. Preferred was the name of the travel agency in Pennsylvania that had booked the band's travel.

"You guess?"

Rob looked at Wynton but said nothing.

"What rate did we get there?" Wynton asked.

Lolis looked up from his seat, sensing from Wynton's tone that he was at least partially serious. The day before Wynton had hand delivered identical letters to both him and Rob. The letters, written by Wynton's manager Ed Arrendell, asked for a better and more prompt written reckoning of day-to-day road expenses.

Wynton suppressed a smile before he again asked Rob a financial question.

"Why didn't we stay at a different hotel in Los Angeles?" he asked again.

"Because the next closest was fifteen minutes from the gig," Rob shot back. "Shit."

In contrast, the Westwood Marquis was just a two-block walk from the Westward Playhouse, where the band gave six concerts in four days. But the Westwood was also very expensive; even steeply discounted, its $600-per-night suites cost more than twice as much as the band typically paid, when the promoter wasn't already paying.

Wynton looked out the window at the Oakland traffic. Hadn't the bus just passed the exit for this weekend's gigs? Wynton remembered from the itinerary booklet that the club where the band was playing was in Emeryville. The bus had just passed a sign that said Emeryville.

"Rob. Where're we staying?" asked Wynton.

"At the Claremont," Rob replied.

"Why we not staying at the Holiday Inn?" A Holiday Inn stood near the exit for Emeryville.

The front lounge was quiet after Wynton's last question. Lolis looked first at Wynton, then at Rob. Almost immediately, however, Wynton broke the apparent standoff.

"Oouu-wheee! Y'all something, boy."

But before anyone had a chance to relax, he started asking more questions.

"Did either of you two gentlemen read that letter from Ed?" he asked.

"I received the letter," said Lolis ceremoniously. "I have not yet had the opportunity to study its contents." Then Rob spoke:

"Shit, man. I know what's in the letter. That letter should never have been sent. Ed should never have sent it. And you should never have endorsed it by giving it to us. That letter's a piece of fucking shit."

"You should tell Ed that so he can whip your ass for you."

"I will. I'll tell him the next time I see him, and I'll enjoy telling him. 'Ed, that motherfucking letter is a piece of bull-shit and you should never have sent it.'"

"Make sure I'm there when you tell him so I can enjoy what comes afterward."

Silence.

"And I'm never opening it, either. And another thing. If you're so concerned about money, if I get you another AT&T

calling card will you use it instead of phoning long distance at hotel rates?"

"Fuck you, Rob."

"Okay, fuck your three thousand dollars in phone calls last month."

"Hey motherfucker, who's paying for this bus you're riding on right now?" Wynton challenged Rob. But then he couldn't maintain the tone, and his anger disappeared. He looked at Rob and started laughing. Soon he and Lolis and Rob were all laughing. The sound of laughter filled the bus as it pulled out of the long driveway leading to the Claremont.

"Lolis, give me forty," said Wynton.

"And you owe me twenty," said Wycliffe.

"Ask Lolis for it, bruh."

One of the reasons Duke Ellington is so great, no matter what happened, he always kept his band going. He'd take what he earned and put it all back into the band. That was a different era. Musicians still complained a lot, but they played a lot softer. When I first got out here, a lot of music industry people thought it was strange that we were playing real jazz. Most of the jazz at that time was fusion or so-called avant-garde. If you wanted to play, Art Blakey and Betty Carter were your only chances to learn. High school and college jazz bands played mainly jazz rock songs, or sanitized "arrangements" of jazz classics. Cats were even wearing jeans on the bandstand as a sign of freedom. When we were first going on the road, Kenny Kirkland said, "I thought we would only be out one week with the type of wild shit we were playing."

As we became more popular, the same older musicians who had been so encouraging when we started became disparaging. Of course they were up against a lot. Rock was very popular, and some of the cats thought you had to find a way to accom-

modate that popularity or become part of it. So our coming out and playing attacked their idea of what they should have been doing. And social critics were even threatened because we dressed up when we played, we tried to be clean. Even though we were so country we'd be wearing things like polyester suits. Damn. Like it wasn't cool to try and look good. But the people kept supporting our jazz. Still do.

Everything Goes On in the World

Packing, looking for my ticket that Billy gave me that I can never seem to find, and the phone is ringing. The phone is always ringing. I like looking down Amsterdam Avenue while I'm talking on the phone, unless I'm at the piano writing some music and talking too. Sometimes I may play something for the person I'm talking with. Clown around and say, "This is called 'Andrea.'" And play something sweet or crazy. Or play a note for each syllable I speak. I imagine the lives of the people speeding up that street, the lights in their cars and trucks bright, where are they all are going, home to girlfriends and boyfriends and to their kids. Going home while I'm leaving mine again.

If we're leaving real early Billy will call me to make sure I'm awake, if I even got to sleep the night before. I don't actually go out a lot when I'm in New York, not to parties. I'll go out to hear someone else play. To see my kids. To see Mr. Murray. Go to a museum. But I almost never go to Broadway shows and movies, unless it's with my youngsters. And never to a disco or something like that. No place that has people lined up. With bodyguards and a man at the door to turn away anyone who doesn't look right.

So Billy calls and it's still dark out, the clock says four A.M. and the driver is coming at four-thirty. Our flight is for around six.

Or it's night. We're going overseas. We go at least once or twice a year, usually in the summer when there are festivals, although lately we've also been going in the fall or spring.

I love watching the streets when we leave for the airport, no matter what time or season. I feel like I'm already outside the city. An objective outsider, impassively observing. I don't stare out the window daydreaming or feeling sad. I talk to the driver. If I know a driver very well, I'll tease him, talk some trash. But if not, just standard conversation.

And then we're crossing one of the bridges and you look back and see the skyline and you know in a few hours you're going to be waking up and this will all be a memory.

"Mr. Winston?"

"Yass?"

Or sometimes it comes out "Morales."

Winston Morales.

Skycaps are the best. They look out for you. "When you coming out with another like that J Mood? That's smooth. Let me see if I can get you an upgrade." There was one brother who worked for an airline who recognized me as the band was sitting down in a plane leaving from Chicago.

"You play saxophone, I know you."

So I nodded. And he asked me, "Who you with?"

"Wynton Marsalis."

"Yeah? He on this flight, too?"

"He's supposed to be. But I think he's late. I think he might miss his flight."

He said, "Well, I love his music. Hope he makes it. What can I give you all? Would you like some champagne?" And about an hour later, just as we were getting into Nebraska, he came back to our seats and presented us with a bottle of champagne. I don't really drink champagne, but we opened that bot-

tle later on the tour, in my hotel room, and some of us drank it next to some barbecue or something similarly redolent of soul, I watched it fizz and listened to it and I saw our plane sitting for two hours on the runway at O'Hare in early winter. I saw my drunken uncle Pete trying to get control of himself to stand up straight. I saw, on a bar stool in Lu and Charlie's club on Rampart Street, Vigor Fisher, a faded, inebriated blues singer, telling me, his eleven-year-old acolyte, "Son, get as much pussy as you can and fuck who don't like it." I saw him trying to slosh his way across the street, only to meet a sober car and an even more sobering concrete grave. I see a look on my father's face and James Black's and John Longo's and Alvin Batiste's and Nat Perrilliat's and all of the musicians' faces that struggled with the reality of this music and this country. That look says, Is this really all we get out of this life? I hear the bubbles cackle and groan and sigh. Jazz in the bittersweet blues of life.

In. Not and.

In London for a concert. I've recorded many baroque CDs with the English Chamber Orchestra here. So every time I come I get a good feeling. I like to go by Hyde Park and hear people standing on boxes, talking shit on various subject, while others stand around and throw their two cents in. There's a great tradition of brass playing here, led by Philip Jones. There was a movement toward jazz by young British musicians in the 1980s. I remember hearing Courtney Pine, Steve Williamson, Julian Joseph in a group called the Jazz Warriors, swinging deep into the night.

I remember walking into a restaurant in London with a gorgeous friend from Greece. Everyone gave me the same look I first saw in a white church in Mississippi, which I was mistakenly taken to by fellow members of a religious retreat in 1974. I left the church but had a good-ass meal in the restaurant. Yup.

A friend of mine from Turkey calls. She is a doctor, in London on business. Wants to come to the concert and talk about us coming to Istanbul. She tells me the British Museum used to have a live Negro from Africa on display. Could I believe that? I said, "Could we still go see him?"

Anyway I was supposed to be working. Not playing that night, but writing. Which I eventually did do, sort of, but until I really get started on something I can procrastinate. It's part of preparing, listening to other music and thinking and talking with people.

JAZZ

Wynton Marsalis Septet & Julian Joseph Quartet
"Impeccable retro from the apotheosis of American jazz trumpet, supported by piano hero Joseph." Royal Festival Hall.

Packed house.
Retro apotheosis!
Leaving very early for Spain. Flying, solo gig, rest of cats meet up day after.

The hotel lobby in London, so quiet at five A.M. A man polishing the wood rail at the bottom of a balustrade. Another dude, balding but with a beard, wearing a double-breasted blue jacket, complaining to a person behind the checkout desk that there was no coffee waiting for him upon his waking up. He was smoking a cigarette as he complained and the ashes spilled onto the desk and the smoke wafted into the eyes of the checkout lady named Vicky, who remained outwardly unperturbed.

We drove in the light rain past the Wellington Monument. Past the slumbering Victoria and Albert Museum. London was looking very tidy, very clean. The traffic around the airport was backed up.

Heathrow Airport. One time I had a driver who spent most of the time from the airport to the hotel arranging business with the other passengers. He said he was married to a woman from the States and they had a child who lived with the mother, the man's wife, back in the States, but for some reason he was driving a cab in London for several months before he rejoined his family. Amazing what people will tell you in a car you'll probably never ride in again. In California this older man told his entire life story on a ride from San Jose to Oakland. He was originally from Wyoming but he spent his adult life in Los Angeles. He went back to Wyoming to take a job as a clerk in a motel that a childhood friend of his owned. Near a ski area. And that's what he did all winter now. One year he went fishing in Wyoming at Thanksgiving in his shirt sleeves, it was so warm. There was no skiing, nobody staying at the motel, so he took off into the mountains. He told me that was the happiest day of his life.

And then he was gone, like most of the rest of the people in my life.

And the amazing thing was he loved Pops. He had about a hundred recordings. All winter in Wyoming while he was working at that inn he listened to some Pops at least once a day.

Seville, Spain—that was our destination from London— Seville at noon was deserted and hot. It was siesta and if you didn't have to be out in the street you weren't. We were staying in an old part of the city a few miles from the airport. There seemed to be no trees at first, the sun just sat up there daring them to grow. Ooouuweeee!

We'd switched planes at Madrid and ran into the Cuban trumpet player Arturo Sandoval, who lives in Florida now, and he was coming from Brazil on his way to the same gig in Seville. While we waited for our connecting flight he took out a piece of wood that had three trumpet valves on it and a mouthpiece and practiced his rapid tonguing and fingering. A lot of musicians like to start something between you and other musicians that play your horn. Saying they said this and that about you and what do you think about it. Sandoval taught me some things about playing low notes. That's what I want to know from a great musician, some information. All that shit-talking and speculation is like asking your woman who she has slept with. You can't do nothing good with that information.

In the lobby of the Melia Seville freshly picked oranges were heaped in a basket.

"Wynton!"

Gerry Mulligan.

We'd just him seen a few weeks before at Ravinia, the great music festival in Chicago. We first played together in the early 1980s, a concert in Seattle. We had a natural musical empathy. He loved to play improvised counterpoint, and so do I. We always had good and sometimes fiery conversations about jazz and race and other things. He was a very honest and direct man. He liked the sound of the band, and was always encouraging me to compose more music. "I heard that naked flat nine at the top of the voicing. That's pretty courageous." He wrote an arrangement of "Broadway" for us and we played it with him.

"We've got to record together," he said. But before we did, he died.

We rode to the gig in a kind of minibus and I sat in the back with some older cats who were playing, too. That always makes me happy, talking to older cats, hearing about their experiences and what it was like to be on the same stage—with Duke, with Count Basie, all of them. And Ray Brown was telling a story about segregation, about not being able to get a room in a hotel in a town somewhere in the South, and he told this story while we drove through the old city, past the Plaza

the sound of laughter 187

des Toros to the expo where we were playing in an outside am-
phitheater that was part of the fair. I told Ray about some of
my own experiences and he said, "Damn, I thought all that
was over by the time you were born."

There was this elaborate security to get backstage, in case of
terrorists. When I finally got to my dressing room I looked at
Rob, who had come with me and said, "What are we playing
this gig for?" And Rob looked at me and shook his head,
dressed to the tens with his mustache well-coiffed, Sugar Rob
just mumbled.

"Fuck if I know."

So I played, nothing but a trumpet gig at the end, a gig
contest Rob called it, with me and then Sandoval and the
others all blowing. No matter how many times you tell your-
self not to start blowing all loud and playing high notes, your
ego always wins and you end up sounding like shit. This
would not be a memorable gig. The people were clapping but
beyond the walls of the amphitheater you could sometimes
hear the music from another part of the fair, you could hear
dance music, and you could imagine the type of public frenzy
that always greets the loud backbeat. When we got off stage I
asked Rob again why the fuck we had come and he said, "A
deuce."

That meant $20,000.

"Should have gotten more."

(But that twenty would help with the bus bill from this
month's tour.)

One of the cats went out dancing later and said he was try-
ing to hook up with a Spanish girl who left for the bathroom
and didn't return and he said it was because she didn't like Ne-
groes. I don't know about that.

Everything goes on in the world.

It was early morning then—the gig hadn't started until after eleven, that's the way they did it there. It was still hot then, too.

Left early next day. Flying to Bilbao to the north. Wrote music whole time on plane. Gig in Vitoria, old Basque town, very close to fighting in the Spanish Civil War. Boy in the car who spoke Basque, knew the history, tried to explain, one town pitted against the next, memories still very strong. I love the promoter of tonight's gig, Iñaki. He works the entire year to present a summer festival and always succeeds in selling tickets and presenting first-class music. Once a year I see him in New York with some good Spanish wine. Iñaki takes care of everyone. He sees to it that you feel at home.

Another homecoming.

We played part of the section of In This House *I had been working on in Virginia. Wess played the living hell out of his sopranino. And there was another section written in Puerto Rico. It was hot there, too, but a different kind of hot, with the ocean right next to where we stayed that night in an ugly room. Puerto Rico, with the window open and hearing the lapping ocean while the moon is quiet witness to wonderful things. The next morning hundreds of kids crowded onto the beach so's you couldn't get to the hotel from front or back because there was a locked gate, and huge waves. I know so many Puerto Ricans in New York, and the feeling here is so much like New Orleans, it doesn't feel like the road. They even have red beans and rice here. Even though they speak the same basic language as the people of Vitoria, Puerto Rico feels like another whole planet. Unless you're at a jazz concert. In Vitoria there was a man in the second row with a black beard and black hair wide-eyed and a woman near him with her eyes closed, her head moving, and I got to say when we finished, "Right now I'd like to bring my father up, Mr. Ellis Marsalis."*

the sound of laughter

He played "The Very Thought of You." Same deep introspective sweet touch as always.

I still get nervous when my father comes to hear us. I don't know why, because he's always supportive. I guess I still wonder whether or not I'm out here representing him properly. All the stuff he showed me, how much of his life he sacrificed for me and my brothers to be out here.

After the concert everyone is hanging out in the hotel jamming and being jammed. Iñaki said from the stage, "This was the concert of the year."

A Call from J.

We never do the same gig twice, in fact "perform" isn't really the right word for what we do because that gives a sense that we're going through a program we've rehearsed, tune by tune, move by move, which isn't what it's like at all.

I never know.

Life's the same. My great uncle who I lived with for a while when I was growing up gave me a stone he had cut that said: DON'T GET DISCOURAGED. *But sometimes you do, or you can feel yourself fighting that wave of discouragement that can come after a bad gig or something you read that gleefully said you weren't shit. And that was the good part. Or a person who let you down. Anything. And you look out the window of your hotel, lights as far as you can see off into the dark distance, and there's that same view a few hours later in the morning, the streets quiet if it's Sunday, with that feeling of ritual that reminds you of childhood. And the phone rings.*

It's the J. Master.

Marthaniel Roberts. Marcus. Damn, he called me from all over before he came out with us. From all over and at all hours. He'd want to talk about our music; he knew it all back then before he started playing with us, this young pianist from Florida. He was so honest and eager to get out here.

When he first started calling, we'd rap for hours. J. is extremely intelligent and likes to get to the bottom of issues. He believes in providing documentation to support his arguments. We would talk about the musical merits of selling out to commercialism, and bring in before and after recordings of our favorite sellouts. We would talk about the European classical avant-garde and its relationship to the jazz avant-garde. From Cecil Taylor to Milton Babbitt. Can a piano be as expressive as a horn? Monk versus Louis Armstrong. Is it some dumb shit to even try and compare the two? Or to compare anything in art? What makes a melody memorable? Beethoven late quartets and the John Coltrane quartet. How differently can four instruments be played? How were they the same? All discussions accompanied by generous CD listening and in-depth dialogue on what is heard.

Once we visited the house where he grew up. There was something in the house that you noticed right away—the type of basic spiritualism that working-class black people had. People who found ways to deal with the unacceptable. I stared at the piano J. played on when he was a little boy. Brought tears to my eyes. We could see little Marcus at that piano, practicing away, still not seeing. When my band broke up, I called J. I don't know why because I didn't really like his playing that much then. But I respected him as a man and loved his pride and mind. Anyway, he came to my apartment in Brooklyn and knew all of our music. That blew my mind. He had learned the music from gig tapes. When he played with us, he knew what I was thinking better than I did. It was difficult to explain, but whatever we were playing he just understood. He said that he would study the style of each soloist in the band. If you hear somebody on the radio today playing the piano with two hands, drenched in the blues, it could only be one thing.

J.

One day we were having lunch in a French restaurant. J. was sitting in with us on a recording. After I'd cut J.'s steak for him and he'd eaten a little bit of it we were talking about a recording, about a tune we'd been playing, and I said, "When we get back in the studio we're going to do one take, J. I don't want to do three or four takes. You don't do fifty takes to get one great solo."

"I just always believe you should do two takes," said J. J. never agrees with you just to be agreeing. He says what's on his mind. Once he asked me, "Man, why do you have to win every argument? Can't you just let a motherfucker be wrong every now and then?"

Then I cut some more of J.'s steak and buttered a piece of bread for him. I started messing with the J.-man about some nonsense.

"Take a woman with a floral dress on, no stockings, what does that mean, J.?"

"That women with floral dresses don't wear stockings." He said it in his uh-huh voice, pretending like he was a contestant on a TV game show.

"And what does that mean, no stockings?"

"Less work later."

J.

It was hot outside. He held my arm while we crossed the street, walking between the usual cars and trucks and taxis. I don't know how most blind people get along in a big, busy city like New York. How do they have the courage to go out onto the street with just a dog and can't see shit? J. says, "Bruh! You learn how to hear and remember where stuff is." Man, I don't know if I could deal with it. "You could if you had to." Something else I learned from J.: The dumbest thing in the world is thinking that *because somebody is blind they automatically become a better musician. J. says, "Let me take your sight and see if your blindness makes you enough of a better musician to balance the loss."*

We took the elevator back up to the studio. Cats were coming back from wherever they'd been, out to eat, back from the hotel for the ones who didn't live in New York. They were staying at a hotel about six or seven blocks from the studio, which the cats liked because it was low key, no sign out front or busy lobby to deal with. In New York I slept at my crib, but I didn't usually go far from the studio during breaks because a taxi to Lincoln Center might take too long if the traffic was heavy.

One time we got J. on the basketball court and he made a few baskets but he wasn't into that so much, or anything that gave him even the slightest feeling that he was being patronized. He is the most sensitive person I have ever known. Subtle changes in attitude, in the silence of a room: He always detected and analyzed them immediately, then gave them the proper response. Four women come backstage after a gig and began talking. One said nothing. When they were finished J. said, "How many women was that?" I said, "Four." He said, "The one who talked the most was overweight, the second one was fine, and the first one was the sister of the one who didn't say anything. The little sister." He was always doing that kind of thing. And damn if he wasn't right almost all the time.

"Okay, this is going to take some concentration, some work, for about thirty-five minutes," I said in the studio. "Everyone get his part out." Everyone but J., of course. He learned his before, listening. Usually I only had to play a new tune for him once and he got it. He could do that, know a tune better than the cats who had the music in front of them that they could see. It was a miracle, I mean some of our music is an hour and a half long and he will know the whole thing in his head. Not

just his part either. Everybody's. We all respected him, his work ethic, his desire.

I didn't like my sound. It had too much attack and not enough sound.

We worked our way through another tune. Maybe my sound was okay after all. Sometimes I don't know. I love working in the studio but I never like the way my trumpet sounds when I hear it played back. Steve gets tired of hearing me complain.

Something else wasn't sounding right.

"Did you do this part?" asked J. And he played it.

"We're coming to that. The next progression is that D flat chord."

"Where are we starting?" asked Swing Doom.

"At the beginning again."

"You mean at that G?"

Damn.

J. interrupted. "That G is supposed to be an A flat."

We worked a long time. You stay in the studio like that and you forget what time it is. What season it is. You work trying to get that tune right and it sounds like shit and the cats are getting tired. I was thinking the piece was going to sound bad, but I was feeling good, too. It's a strange thing to explain. Partly it was be-ing in the studio, just knowing that as long as we stayed in there that's all we would do: play. But it was also what we were play-ing, even when it didn't sound like it should—except later, when the tapes came from Steve Epstein, there was a good take after all, and we used it—but even when we were sounding ter-rible because the music was hard, you would still be thinking, yes, because jazz music is affirmative, because the blues is affir-mative, because the swing teaches you to negotiate the stormy seas of collaboration. But even above that, you would be think-ing yes, yes. Play good enough and you never die.

Yes.

By nine o'clock, over three hours since we had returned from our last break, we were still working.

"Concentrate. The fast tempo is not fast enough. Shit, it's not that hard."

Another half hour passes. During a playback, Homey dances, sliding on the floor in his sandals. Then Reginald pretends he is a ballet dancer.

"Did you hear that?" asks one of the men.

"Yeah."

"I messed it up," the guilty player continues.

"That's okay. Did you mess it up every take?"

"Yeah, I think so."

"That's okay. Just the sound, the music, that's what I want."

Then it was time for us to go. We'd been in the studio eleven, twelve hours. But J. and I stayed on.

It felt good to be playing with J. We had a dialogue that never stopped, a dialogue through music about living in the world. But one day J. called me.

"Skain?"

And the way he said it, with just a little break in the inflection right at the end where his voice should have been going up still if he was going to tell me another story, right off there wasn't any doubt what he was going to say next, there'd never been really from when he began, someday he'd have to be on his own. Later, after he left, we hit some rocky spots in our relationship. Still, there is something that binds us that will never be broken. I learned so much from him and him from me. Whenever we play, we feel the love and all those years of nights trying to make sense of our lives through this glorious music. Still, J.

Yes.

Harold Russell.
  Harold Russell!
  Harold. Ha-rold.
  Russell.
  Ooouuweeee, Harold!
  Harold.

"Where's my trumpet at, Wes?" Wynton called out.

A huge man from Buffalo, New York, bigger than Warm Daddy, this Wes used to be the equipment manager for the San Francisco Giants. He had hooked up briefly with the band on a New England tour. Wes had also worked for rock bands and several other pro baseball teams.

As he toted Wynton's horn along a hotel hallway in Boston, the time almost eight o'clock, Wes told a couple of jokes and kidded Wynton about his haircut. Not long after, in the dressing room, instead of warming up, Wynton gave a student who had managed to sneak in an impromptu, thirty-second lesson. Then he played a few notes, the anticipation that has been building all day bursting.

"This trumpet sounds wrong," he said. But he didn't panic; there was no last-minute loss of composure, though he could be short with someone who happened to be near.

"I think it needs to be cleaned," Wynton continued, though he knew there was no time for that then.

He played a few more notes, asking one of the other musicians to listen. Homey nodded in agreement that something indeed didn't sound right, but Wynton let it go. No one in the hall would notice.

"You like that?" I may smile to someone as I come off the stage afterwards. But that is the only admission I will make that I know we've played well.

"Man, that's music," an older man at a club murmured to his companion the other night, loud enough for me to overhear. It made me feel good, not just to hear his praise, but to know that our music made him happy.

Something seemed wrong in the second set a few nights later. Wynton didn't think he was playing well. He stopped to talk. Maybe words would cure.

"You don't learn about us in school," he began, after soloing in "The Very Thought of You." "Jazz music is not necessarily the most popular thing in the world. I feel grateful I can play for you."

Harold! Where are you, Harold?

Mr. Russell. Mr. Harold Russell.

The band was back in Seattle to play some jazz. We'd come to Seattle from Oregon, where the band had played three gigs in three days in Monmouth, Jacksonville, and Portland. Spokane before that. In the two weeks since a long weekend Wynton spent at a music festival in Greensboro, North Carolina, they'd also played on *The Tonight Show*, at Friday Harbor on San Juan Island and at Orcas Island, both in Puget Sound, and in Vancouver and Victoria, British Columbia.

Earlier that month they had made a record in New York City.

They had played another weeklong engagement at the Village Vanguard in New York, during which they also recorded enough music for another album that would become part of a seven–CD boxed set.

After Seattle they would play more gigs in California. Then a week of performing in New York. Then three days in France. Back to New York. On to the Midwest. Then a long South American tour, a month in Europe, a month in the West and South.

While the band was touring Wynton practiced. In his hotel room, on the bus. One long night on the bus he practiced in his bunk with a mute on his trumpet. It was three A.M.

"Harold, would you please turn the damn air conditioning down!"

"You got it buddy. Wyn-ton. Brother Wynton."

Wynton gave a few workshops. He put off writing some music he was supposed to be writing, but he thought about it a lot. He tried chords, played with some melodies. He played ball, talked on the phone, watched CNN, rapped with Leebo.

Leebo had been backstage with the band, too, before the men went on. Veal had started something on the bass and then Homey picked it up, a Seattle calypso, and Homey started dancing. He was always dancing. If you're going to play the drums you must be able to dance, and Homey could dance. Homey could also play basketball. And he used to play trumpet. That's how he'd begun his musical life, on the trumpet, playing in parades in New Orleans.

It must have been after four o'clock before we went on that afternoon outside Seattle.

The night before in Portland, Wynton and Wess and Wycliffe and Homey wanted to play some more so they went to a club called the Hobbitt where Teddy Edwards was headlining on sax. Teddy Edwards was almost old enough to be Wynton's grandfather, but he was still youthful-looking, handsome. The men walked into the club late, after midnight, and just started playing. The air was smoky, the light dark. A woman in the audience came up and started singing.

Parades and picnics.

It was hot that day in Seattle. And Wynton was wearing a white suit. Standing on that stage, his life in a phrase, in the tone.

The great tenor saxophonist Charlie Rouse, who had played so much music with Monk, played in our band the summer of 1987. He would hear us practicing and talking about music, talking about new ways to play—harmonic and rhythmic approaches, ways to write complex forms that still sounded good. He said, "All of that is good but that's what music is. Harmony, rhythm, form. The something new is not in what you play. It's in yo' sound, baby. It's in yo' sound." He looked deep inside of me when he said it so I would understand it, feel it, and remember it with the same intensity that he delivered it.

When Miles was really playing, back before he got into all that fusion thing, that money thing, before all that, when he played he had such a sound. He could be playing just one note and it was the blues, just the sound he made.

The band played two encores, then another. Still the people kept clapping and hollering. Wynton knew from Rob that the promoter was getting worried about how he was going to pay overtime to the people backstage if the audience never left. So Wynton looked at Warm Daddy.

"What should we do?" he asked.

"Play a ballad," replied Wess.

Afterwards people came and talked with Wynton by the stage. He signed a CD cover. And an old album.

He signed someone's hand.

The label on a bottle of wine.

Then a boy who'd been holding Wynton's new trumpet tried to play it.

"Don't play too loud," cautioned Wynton.

The boy tried again.

"Listen to music," said Wynton. "When you listen, you get an idea of what it takes to speak. It's like a baby learning to talk. Before you play, have an idea of what you're going to play. Then play in phrases."

The boy tried again. It was still warm out. People on blankets were still drinking wine, hugging each other, thinking perhaps of when they got home tonight. A girl gave Wynton a plate of homemade chocolate chip cookies. And the boy on the trumpet played some more.

"You have a good rhythmic imagination," said Wynton encouragingly.

Suddenly an older man started heckling him, saying how great Miles Davis had played the last time he'd heard him.

Wynton glanced in his direction while continuing to listen to the boy. *What he said didn't bother me. People say all kinds of things. But why did he have to do that when this youngster was trying to play?*

Wynton signed another autograph. *Smiled and nodded like a psychiatrist, said "Yes, he was great."*

"It's nice to meet you, too. You're looking so clean. And you have a beautiful girlfriend."

Picture posing.

Where's my horn?

"Hey, Rob, we going? What time is it?"

The band took the bus back to the hotel and changed and drove to a park where there were some hoops. One of the musicians left to buy drinks at a store. Kids shouted from a Little League baseball game in the park, with lights in its field and a real outfield fence. The musicians could hear the kids playing baseball as they shot baskets, and the lights from the ballfield lit the court. The men played a long time. Wynton's finger was hurting from where he'd broken it in another game. Nothing to do but keep playing. Wynton had to call Delfeayo when he got back to the hotel. It was Delfeayo's birthday. A pianist who wanted to play had been trying to reach Wynton. During a break in the game, Leebo told the band about a New Orleans gig when he and Wynton were getting paid according to the number of people who came; one person came so they got twenty-five cents.

They told stories about Leebo's brother-in-law Botchie, who was the percussionist in their funk band. Botchie died when his house caught fire.

Rob said he never noticed Mt. Rainier during the gig. And he was practically staring right at it.

The bus to take us to California was parked by the Wendy's I could see from my hotel window the next morning.

You do something so often, over and over, it becomes you. And the amazing thing, it wasn't there before you did it and of course will be gone afterwards, yet while you're doing it . . . how do I express this?

Once in Lincoln, Nebraska, but it could have been anywhere, we played a tune, "You Don't Know What Love Is," which we play often, always different but always that tune. And that night in Lincoln, cold as a motherfucker outside, we'd just flown in from New York, the cats were just getting back together, and that night when we played "You Don't Know What Love Is" I was thinking about the feeling of someone laughing, it could be a little boy or girl down the street that you hear as you're sitting on your steps in the evening, or a woman on the phone thousands of miles away and you've just said something that made her happy, or one of your kids in the bathtub. Someone laughing. And I was thinking about that as we got to the end of the song and I started playing around with some fourths, intervals of fourths, and I played maybe one minute, I wasn't counting, just all different fourths. Then the song ended.

After the gig a person spoke to me about that song. "Man, you were playing some shit there, all those fourths," something like that is what he said. He wanted to talk about the fourths. He had all these questions about them. How many had I played? Had I ever done that before? Wasn't that a new way for me to end that tune? And so on.

"I was just thinking about the sound of laughter."

The color of her eyes.

The light off the river downtown looking across to Algiers, Louisiana.

Fear.

The way the living room smelled in my first girlfriend's house.

When she hugged me.

That funeral I flew home for. Crazy night, High Point went with me and we had to change planes in Dallas. It felt like we were on the plane all night and then coming back all day, but the feeling of being there for that service. . . . It is hard to explain.

Once we were in Philadelphia for a gig and my first girlfriend from when I was growing up had all the cats over for dinner. It felt so good being in that apartment, eating that good food together, and she was so glad to see us. We talked about all kinds of things. She has a corporate job in a chemical company but wants to start her own business. I always encourage her to go on her own. "Do your own. You never get the time back. It's like playing your own stuff when you solo. Always play your own." She was just glad to see us and wanted us to enjoy the New Orleans feast she had been preparing for us all week. The warmth of her arms around my shoulders. Her hands on my head. She's going to do her own.

Something I knew and loved, ever since I can remember . . .

*. . . Alvin Batiste, Wess's college teacher, who grew up with
E., invited us to do a workshop at Southern University in Baton Rouge. He had his band there. They could* play. *Then he
introduced me. He's a man of enormous intelligence and dignity, and warmth. An unbelievable musician, constantly in the
woodshed. He was happy we were there. He just loves Wess.
You could tell just the way he said our names. We were home.
Or the gig we did every year at Blues Alley in Washington, a
long ride from the hotel through those Washington streets that
always seem empty late at night. Where do all the people who
work for the government go at night? And you really do go
down this little alley to get to the club, and it's so crowded in
there, the dressing room is real tiny, it feels close and good.*

*We would go to Blues Alley every year, in the winter usu-
ally. The club is up in the Georgetown section. It has the tiniest stage, maybe just a little bigger than the Village Vanguard
but very small.*

*"You don't know what love is until you know the meaning
of the blues." That's the whole first line of that song.*

*Of course we played it sometimes in Blues Alley, but all
through the Eighties we used to set the club on fire. Every
year we would see the same fans. We recorded live there
many years ago so we could always remember the feeling of
that place and that time.*

"Do you play any serious music, or just jazz?"

That was the question Dr. Sloan Hales had asked one of
the musicians at his ranch, the Wyoming Hereford Ranch, in
Cheyenne, Wyoming. *I let it go. He was our host.* Wynton
wasn't able to go to the lunch Dr. Hales and his wife Anna
Marie had for the men, but he met them later. They were
Mormons. Their ranch was so big it had its own exit on the
interstate highway that ran by Cheyenne. Thousands of
acres. The house had two grand pianos and a pipe organ in

the living room, so the Haleses could have concerts for their friends. All the Hales children played the piano and the organ. Dr. Hales, too. He was also a mountain climber. And he still practiced medicine, working as an anesthesiologist at the hospital in Cheyenne.

We left a serious feeling in Cheyenne.

It was spring on the plains, the grass still sere, the mountains in the distance all snow-covered, but the air had the smell of warmth and moisture, melting and growing.

Dr. Cedric Reverend books the concerts at the University of Wyoming in Laramie. He is an august professor of English, a man of sharp wit and refined taste. We never know where he'll show up. London once in the summertime. He sent me an excellent reading list. I want him to enjoy our music. He is a discerning critic and responsible for bringing a new world of art to Wyoming.

Harold had stopped for a special permit when the bus crossed into Wyoming at Laramie. Miss Darlene was traveling with the band, too. *She always sent Harold out with some good cake or banana bread for us. Always fixed a good home-cooked meal for us in Nashville.*

We were only in Laramie overnight. It was Miss Darlene's last night with us. She'd been on her vacation and now she had to fly home to Tennessee. Harold would be putting her on the plane in Cheyenne, after the band arrived at an inn that had a nine-hole golf course that went all the way around the rooms, with trees, and beyond the course the plains. People playing golf could see buffalo grazing.

It was Miss Darlene's birthday and the band had a little party for her on the bus. Harold made a video of the party they had for her. Then he ran the video again, with her help, on the bus to Cheyenne. The band was late leaving Laramie, on account of the party. The men played "Happy Birthday."

Heading east out of Laramie, through Medicine Bow National Forest, the silver and lavender bus passed antelopes in the mountains. Some of the men watched a nature video on the VCR in the front of the bus. Then Warm Daddy put some tapes on. He always brought tapes with him on the bus, and CDs. Hardly a day went by that we didn't listen to some Coltrane or Monk or something else that Wess had picked out for us. And Rob always had a tape of the last performance. Wess liked to put those on, too. He sat up front, next to Harold, since they were the only two who smoked. Except when Miss Darlene was along. Then she got the seat by her husband. The men called her the co-pilot. She would talk to Harold or read. Miss Darlene said she sometimes read as many as fifteen Harlequin romances a week.

In Cheyenne the spring feeling was still in the air but it was not the same as the morning. The band had a gig to play, after that late lunch at the ranch. Wynton had music he had to keep writing. *You do something so often, over and over, but each time is different, too, imagine that morning in the middle of that country where so many men and women had died, slaughtered like the Herefords the Hales raised or the buffaloes.*

The sound of laughter.

And a little while before the band had been in another part of the country, in Mississippi, where scenes of a different slaughter had been commonplace when Wynton's father and mother started having their family. *I was alive then.* The slaughtering of people's aspirations because other people didn't want them to go to a certain school. Separate sections of seats on the bus, at the soda fountain. *I always wonder how my mother, with her deep intelligence and high-mindedness, could handle growing up 'till she was in her twenties under Jim Crow. How did that affect who she came to be.*

The sound of laughter.

The bus came into Mississippi fast. Wynton was sitting up front with Harold and Warm Daddy.

"Warrrrm Daddy!" That was Harold talking.

Harold was driving fast, through an area of pine trees, like you might see in Georgia. The trees lined both sides of the road. Harold was worrying about his radar detector. He didn't want to get stopped. On the stereo Wess had chosen a ballad, the kind of ballad Wynton's mother would like. *That's what she always liked, slow ballads.*

It was cold outside, in the thirties.

Wynton and Lolis had been going over plans for an NPR radio series, *Making the Music*, while Wynton was writing some more of a new commission. The twenty-six-part series, which looked at how jazz is made, would win a Peabody Award. *There was some wild stuff in the piece. New rhythms. I was at the part of writing it where I had the whole structure in my mind and I was just filling it in now. Themes. Modulations. Turned-around rhythms.*

Lolis was working on his computer in the back of the bus while Wynton and Wess and Harold watched the pine trees on the road and listened to the music. *If Wess was playing that tune he'd probably play thirteen choruses if we let him.*

Sometimes I wonder who notices. Sometimes my faith is tested. It's not like when I was first out here and very few people were hearing anything non-commercial. Now, though, there were still those days when you wondered. I went to visit a high school in New York. It's one of those schools where adults have given up. The kids are out of control. And the level of ignorance is profound.

So the only thing to do was get up and keep working. Get up, eat breakfast, get on the bus, and drive to Mississippi.

After a while it's easy to succumb to the routine. Just another school, just another gig. But every step of the way you have to deal with each thing you do. You can't just slide over this gig or not hear that person. You've got to remember to feel each experience and invest the energy to make it glorious.

"Talked to J. last night for an hour. He says to tell you what's happening."

I'd never write thirteen choruses for Wess. And for some of the cats I never have to write a real part at all. And I don't.

Just then Veal was making another of his special sandwiches. He took his time making it like he did when he was getting dressed or just before he went out on stage, checking his profile. If he had to hurry to make a sandwich he'd skip it.

"Oh I'm going fishing when I get home to Atlanta," Veal sang out. He talked like that, singing almost, in his deep bass voice.

"Pass me the milk, bruh.

"Hey Harold, can you hit the switch for the microwave? Thanks, bruh.

"Any of those sardines in that cupboard?

"Shit, who made this coffee?"

Highway 45 ran through the middle of Columbus, Mississippi. The band was staying at the Holiday Inn on the outskirts, near the interstate exit. A sign said:

WELCOME WYNTON MARSALIS AND ENSEMBLE

The motel didn't have any suites, so Wynton was put in an outbuilding that was for newlyweds. Two rooms, one with a TV, and the other with a piano.

A man wearing an L.L.Bean jacket came into the motel lobby. One of the musicians asked what was L.L.Bean. And

the sound of laughter

the man explained there was a store in Maine. And then he said did one of the musicians know where they had jackets with a lapel emblem that said L.L.Coon?

The sound of laughter.

On the other side of Highway 45, down the road a piece, was a section of shanties. Some were built on stilts. An old black man waved to the musicians as they passed him on the way to "The W."

"The W" was further past the fancy section of town. "The W" was the nickname of a school called Mississippi University for Women, though it was coed now. The novelist Eudora Welty had gone to school there for a year, and the school had named a building after her. One of the professors told Wynton there had been a debate about the band's coming. "Even though we are in the heart of the blues," he said, "country is still king in this area."

The hall was packed for the concert. The head of the local telephone company introduced the band, talking in exclamation points. He'd brought eight people with him to the concert! He thanked all the concert patrons! He had sunglasses with him and now he was going to put them on and listen to some jazz!

The band started with "New Orleans Function." The windows in the hall were open and Wynton heard a train whistle. He tried to match his trumpet pitch to the pitch of the whistle, which was in fourths.

The sound of laughter.

"This tune commemorates the passing of the deceased into the earth, from whence he came," Wynton explained. "Then we celebrate the continuation of life."

Afterwards, some folks introduced themselves to Wynton as being from "up north, from Shreveport."

Then the musicians went to a party in a mansion built before the Civil War. There were many antebellum mansions in this section of Columbus. Supply lines during the war had moved through the next town, and the mansions had been saved. Now, nearly a hundred and fifty years later, the mansions were such an attraction that there was an annual open house in which you could go visiting from one mansion to the next.

The ceilings in the mansion the band visited were fifteen feet high. The party was in the band's honor, but not all the men could make it. Some were tired, others just wanted to be alone, without the burden of socializing after a performance. A waiter served sandwiches, rich brownies, and white wine. The gracious hostess talked about herself and her home and her love of music. Then she and Wynton sat at the table in her kitchen and talked past midnight.

The next morning Wynton missed breakfast before the band left for Jackson, Mississippi, where Wynton gave a workshop for two hundred students at Millsaps College.

At the students' request he played the trumpet. He played "Embraceable You," accompanying himself on the piano.

Up in one of the last rows of seats of that modern hall sat an older woman Wynton had never met. She had read about the workshop in the local paper. Her father used to play the cornet in a marching band. He had been dead for forty years. His daughter, this woman at the workshop, didn't go out at night, so when she read about the workshop she came because she couldn't come to the concert, which began at eight.

She asked Wynton to demonstrate triple tonguing, and he obliged. Triple tonguing required the ability to articulate triplets clearly and evenly by a learned sequence of tongue movements. It was easier to illustrate by playing part of

"Carnival of Venice." Every student who wants to call himself a trumpet player tries to learn it. Wynton played it as a boy in New Orleans.

"That meant the world to me," said the woman. "My father used to play that."

Jazz in the bittersweet blues of life.

The band had no soundcheck scheduled that afternoon. Rob was busy with some lights he'd rented, but the musicians played anyway.

Runout

Late June, a Sunday, in New York. Harold had parked the bus a block up from the hotel, which was not the hotel the band was in when they came to town. But the promoter of their gig the previous night had paid for the hotel, and he'd chosen a different one. So everyone in the band had to move. There was some grumbling. Now the musicians were going on a runout, a one-night stand from which they would return after the gig. Just bring your instrument and a change of clothes for the concert.

The bus was full. High Point had come along and he'd brought his two daughters. Also along for the ride was a saxophone player Wynton met in Australia, named Andrew, and Wynton's friend Amy.

"This bus is a model U.N.," said Rob.

"Did you see your picture in *The Times*?" Amy asked Wynton.

"Nope," said Wynton.

The drive lasted about an hour. The band was playing in a large white tent with the sides open on the grounds of an arboretum, with lawns all around and a greenhouse. Rob said he needed the band for about a five-minute soundcheck, but everyone played for half an hour. Andrew from Australia joined in. Then there was a workshop at five.

"The blues is a classic American form," Wynton said at the workshop. "Let me show you on the piano, twelve bars.

"What jazz musicians do is play with it, play with the form. Now I'll do it on the trumpet. Now with Wycliffe, we're going to play with each other. Interact.

"There are different devices we use. One is call and response, say I'll play and Wycliffe will answer. Another is riff, something repeated over and over. And polyphonic improvisation, which is the way jazz most resembles democracy.

"Imagine a city where the streets are laid out symmetrically like graph paper. This is like the blues form. Twelve bars of equal length repeated over and over again.

"Another thing is the conception of virtuosity.

"These days most of what we hear is based on a beat. Whereas a groove is organic. When we're playing, we're playing in an interaction, in a groove. It's like a good conversation. A beat is static, it doesn't change. Machines play it.

"In a groove, the interactions change. So the groove develops, which is organic. And that's what jazz music comes out of. Diversity.

"A few other things. There's the break. That's when everyone stops and you're left to go for whatever you know. Be ready for the break, you're on your own."

It was a talk Wynton had given several hundred times, around the world. The talk was never the same, though he covered the same kinds of things. Often he spoke at schools, poor schools in the city where the teachers were struggling to keep going. Or famous universities, many of which had given him honorary degrees, though he never went to college.

I played some blues for those kids that night at the gig. I hope High Point took some good pictures of them, though he was busy watching his girls. They lived with their mother, and High Point had them on weekends, every other weekend maybe. He loved them. They were always going on trips with him. He took them to Memphis, where he was born, and Chicago, where he grew up, and Marciac with us, and all over.

People who think we're just out here having a good time don't know. You have to find your good time.

Each of us has been through some shit to be out here. You didn't just say, "I'm going on the road," and leave. You have to deal with things. Homey supported two families, his and his dead sister's. Warm Daddy, whose only sister was shot and killed by her husband, who also killed their little son. Wess was playing in a club when it happened and they had to tell him afterwards, his wife Desi did. He never talks about it. What is there to say about it? He plays. He plays.

five

What's this note tucked into the door? A card? A business card? No message, nothing, just his business card.

No sleep with my son Jasper last night. Staying at his mother's house. Maurice along with me. Calls himself Cousin Maurice. He's not really my cousin, but he sure can cook him some gumbo.

Maurice.

And tell great lies. You want to know about the lower frequency of men and how they relate to each other? Lies, competition and jealousy. Matt Dillon used to say a friend is one who loves you and one who pipes you.

So Swig doesn't even say goodbye before catching his plane? Brings his son who lives out here in L.A. to the gig last night and this morning, Sunday morning, he's gone.

Wonder what all those folks in the Hollywood Bowl made out of Big Train. Oouuee, that was a long piece to play for them! Damn!

Can somebody tell me? Can somebody please tell me? Oh where, oh where, does the big train go?

jazz in the bittersweet blues of life

"Doesn't anybody on this bus have some cards?"

No, Miss Lee.

She was a dancer, a close friend of one of the men in the band who had traveled with us before, in California. She was the only woman on the bus today. She called each of us "Darling." Or sometimes she addressed us all, with a sweep of her hand and a purr in her alto voice: "My darlings."

Miss Lee was looking for a deck of cards to play solitaire. She had actually found a deck at the hotel, before the bus left Atlanta early in the afternoon, but she had forgotten them. No cards on the bus, but lots of snacks, which were plentiful and high in cholesterol. Bologna and other cold cuts, a stack of American cheese, with each slice wrapped individually, the frozen chicken wings that Cone loved to heat up in the microwave and eat a whole package of. Cone did that with microwave popcorn, too. Ate the whole bag and made some more.

Cone. Coupe de Cone.

"My darlings. No one has any cards. No one wants to play. So. I'm going to make some of my good coffee."

Sitting at the table in the front lounge, Miss Lee munched on a pear that came in a basket of fruit from the dressing room at another gig. By contract with concert promoters, the band always had a prescribed variety of food and drink in its dressing room. The band's friends in the cities and towns where they played also sent cookies backstage or cake, or fruit. A note on a basket might say, "Mr. Marsalis, Welcome to Omaha," or something personal, "Dear Wynton, My wife and I were married to 'Hot House Flowers.'" These notes, too, were collected if someone remembered. They might be gathered after a gig into a fruit basket, with letters and other mementos, including photographs, so that someone looking for an apple or banana on the bus the next morning would find the mail there as well. Then, these souvenirs would go along with the band, to be read and reread by anyone sitting at the table as the men traveled across the country.

On this short trip on a Saturday afternoon, half the band was napping, and two men were in the rear lounge watching a video. Wynton was in his bunk before the bus departed Atlanta's city limits, having slept last night only from about seven A.M. until ten. Because he had sushi for lunch, and because the trip started at the odd hour of two-thirty P.M., he skipped the Cocoa Krispies and climbed right into his bunk, with its own sheets, a blanket, a curtain, air conditioner and heater vent, a little lamp, and about twelve inches of head room.

Wynton's fatigue, which would disappear when he walked on stage, came not just from too little sleep but also the game of touch football the musicians had played in the hotel parking lot. *Georgia spring, buds on trees, dirt roads and shanties in a trailer park only a few miles from the mall.* In the forty-eight hours or so since the band had arrived in Atlanta, midway on a three-week swing through several southern states, Wynton had been the guest of honor at an art reception, during which he also jammed with the reception band. He'd appeared before the Georgia State Senate to receive a citation, lectured before a large crowd at Spelman University, done a few interviews, and, just last night, played two sets at the Roxy Theater. The logistics of all these events had been arranged, deftly as always, by Ed Arrendell. *Ed was always behind the scene. That the septet could stay on the road and remain economically viable was a testament to the genius of Ed. He was raised in Philly and possesses a Harvard M.B.A., but is not above kicking some tail if that is needed. I rely on Ed as I do no one or nothing else. Ed was at the foundation of everything we did on the road.*

Soon the drone of the huge diesel engine changed pitch as the bus changed gears, coming up a hill into Athens, Georgia. The sound signaled someone from inside the Georgia Theater to come out, where he directed the bus into its space, marked by a few orange plastic cones in the street. The man from the theater hollered over the din to the short man behind the wheel with gray hair and wire-rimmed glasses wearing a T-shirt and smoking a cigarette. Harold had his window open and was hollering back to the man from the theater. The two men's voices echoed down the hill.

"Couldn't find the damn directions!" said Harold, his voice rising in pitch with each word. "Knew when I saw the street I'd know where I was!"

Darlene Russell, down from Nashville for a weekend with her husband, said, "Look at that girl in the blue vest, Harold. Isn't she cute?"

Darlene looked cute, too, in her matching white sweats, with the name of her home state of Colorado printed across the front.

"Why, that old Ford, that's a '49," Harold said, snacking on one of the homemade brownies Darlene had brought with her from Nashville. "Look at that, Miss Darlene. Worked on one with my brother. Restored it."

Athens was a quiet southern university town situated on a hill. The University of Georgia campus held dominion over the landscape of expansive lawns, tree-shaded sidewalks, and turn-of-the-century buildings. The whole scene evoked the idealized image of a simpler, slower era. On this Saturday afternoon in early spring an occasional student poked his head out the door of a bar, but almost everyone appeared to be away for the weekend. By the side entrance of the theater, a fraying old movie house converted into a nightclub, someone fussed with the chain on his ten-speed bicycle. A young woman carrying a boom box crossed at the corner and sauntered toward the theater's kiosk to buy a ticket for the band's show that night.

As soon as Harold had the bus in place, its door swung open and a procession of people began to emerge. Rob pushed off first. He had the air of a man on a mission, someone who was not to be interrupted unless the matter was urgent and important.

"Toon Yab!" a voice from inside the bus beckoned after Rob. "Toon Yab Scab! Toon!" Rob smiled, knowing that the person calling him was trying to break his concentration, probably by calling attention to the pretty girl walking by. But he didn't turn his head.

Music came from the bus, a CD of Duke's "Diminuendo and Crescendo in Blue." Someone yelled, "Wake up, Swing Doom!"

Reginald had been sleeping since the bus left Atlanta. His hightop Nikes, always carefully cleaned, lay on the floor below his top bunk. Coming through the door that separated the bus bunks from the front lounge, Reginald was sleepy and hungry.

"Hey, Skizzaine," he said to Wynton. "You know where we are, bruh?"

Wynton did not reply to Reginald's question, really a form of address, even if in fact Reginald had forgotten where the band was playing.

Though Reginald was certainly used to traveling like this, catching an hour or two of sleep whenever he could, rarely sleeping more than five or six hours at one stretch, he still didn't like it. He wanted to stay at home with Kim and their young children.

Carrying his trumpet in a black nylon case, held by a short strap over a shoulder, Wynton stepped outside. He was wearing a T-shirt and blue pleated pants with ribbed cuffs. In the warm air, a couple with two young children were waiting for him. The woman and he had been to high school together.

It seemed perfectly natural to Wynton that he would have such a chance encounter here. His life was a continuous series of remarkable meetings, big and small. Just a few days ago, in Florida, a total stranger had introduced himself to Wynton after a concert with the confessions that both his children had been born to Wynton's music.

A student on a bicycle stopped when he recognized Wynton.

"How do you shift this?" Wynton asked him.

Then Wynton handed his trumpet to the startled bike owner and climbed onto the bike.

"I'll be right back," he promised.

Wynton rode around the block, passing underneath the theater marquee with its lights blinking in the dusk around the words WYNTON MARSALIS, SAT. Seeing that made him feel good because it meant there was a show in town that people were getting ready to come to right now.

A few minutes later, Wynton was inside the theater, which smelled of stale smoke and sweat from last night's Live Championship Wrestling. He noticed two bars in the back, underneath the balcony. A sign, WELL BRANDS $2.50, CALL BRANDS $3.50. The owner of the theater, Kyle Anderson, told Wynton when the band was here last year that the building was once the town's YMCA and later a department store. Kyle's mother cooked a delicious dinner for the band, one the men still talked about. They were looking forward to a return visit today, after soundcheck.

"That was a terrible spree!" they said to one another.

The band also visited the home of Wycliffe in nearby Augusta, and Wycliffe's mother also cooked a memorable dinner. They would not be visiting Augusta this time, but everyone remarked on being again in the state whose predominant tree inspired Wycliffe's nickname.

"Coupe deee Cone!" Wynton called to Wycliffe.

Wycliffe nodded as he continued playing the bass; the men often switched instruments, usually just for fun, but Wycliffe could actually play the bass. Since joining the band, Wycliffe had matured rapidly into a musician of immense technical invention and emotional expression. But for all the growing sophistication of his art, he retained his boyish sense of humor.

The joke in the band this week was that Wycliffe was just learning to read. Not notes, but words. Wycliffe played his dimwit's role with style, pretending that he had trouble talking, too.

"Awaja, waja, waja, it?" he asked someone with mock seriousness. And then he answered his own question, "Ohchu, acka, malaladodoboood."

It was a fine display, one we had enjoyed before and were certain to be given the opportunity to do so again.

With the other band members, Wycliffe waited now for direction from Wynton.

"Pipe in the bucket!" someone hollered, in an indelicate reference to one of Wynton's lesser known compositions, a kind of musical tribute to intimate human interaction. The phrase was sometimes used in conversation as a kind of Zen-like answer to a variety of questions: How are you? Where are you going? What time is it?

Pipe in the bucket.

Though Wynton laughed along with the jokes, internally he was already beginning the preparations for tonight's performances, making observations that came automatically after so many years of playing his horn in public. *My chops feel tight tonight. Remember to call Cone's tune. Lighting's a little dim in here.* Soon it would be time for soundcheck, but Rob wasn't ready for the musicians just yet. He was still setting up. There were no music stands with lights, which meant the men would not be able to rehearse a long piece that required printed parts. This might also limit the selection of tunes Wynton could call, since the band was using a substitute pianist tonight, a young man from St. Louis named Peter.

Wynton placed his horn on the floor of the stage and peered over Peter's shoulders. The stage was small, almost like a nightclub stage. *I love playing in buildings like this. They have a practical feeling to them, like a high school or college gym. Being in the Georgia Theater reminds me of places I played in years ago.*

Another homecoming.

Wynton had known Peter since Peter was a junior-high-school student and Wynton appeared as soloist with the St. Louis Symphony in the Haydn Trumpet Concerto. Peter's father was a violinist in the orchestra. That first time Wynton met Peter, he was called Pete. Pete played all kinds of piano on a blues. He would later call and play McCoy's entire solo from "Lonnie's Lament," on Coltrane's *Crescent*. Hardly high school fare. Peter's best school friend was Todd Williams, the Deacon.

Since Wynton first came to New York young musicians have been living with him, calling, coming over for advice, or just to get a feeling. Pete was one of them. He came to New York to attend Juilliard, but after a year or so he decided the city wasn't for him. He moved to New Orleans, where he had been trying to support a wife and two young children on his earnings as a jazz pianist. Before coming out on the road for this part of the tour, Pete learned all of Wynton's music by heart.

"When you're playing and you hear someone opening up, then you have to open up," Wynton said to Peter, who was working on the difficult stride solo in "Jungle Blues," an eighty-year-old Jelly Roll modal tune the band had played every night this week. Peter tried another passage. Wynton spoke to all his musicians like this, at one point or another. *If you take it personally, you don't understand what we're doing.*

When Wynton was first sitting in with bands in New York, back when he was still a student at Juilliard, he was subbing on a Broadway show and didn't understand how the music was written. It soon became clear that he didn't know the tunes.

"Hey!" the bandleader said. "Somebody get that kid the fuck off the bandstand!" And that was it. No gig. *You have to be prepared. You never know when that chance might be your only chance.*

"You can't force a rhythm to swing," Wynton continued now. "You have to let the swing." *This was severe criticism if a cat misunderstood its intent. But I was only trying to make the music better. And to help Peter grow. I love Pete. He knows this. I hope he knows it.*

"And another thing, use the whole range of the piano, the bottom and the top."

Peter kept playing. He demonstrated that he understood what Wynton was saying to him. Peter was a very fine jazz pianist. What he was mastering now may be the hardest thing of all.

"Soundcheck!" Rob's voice interrupted.

It was nearly six o'clock, time for only one tune, Duke's "Play the Blues and Go." The band played just part of it and then left by bus for dinner at the home of Kyle's mother, Lee Anderson.

Lee's house overlooked a river in the wooded hills outside Athens. It was not a house Wynton could imagine living in— *I like living in the city, feeling the energy of many people*—but he had no trouble appreciating Lee Anderson's happiness in it. A widow, she had insisted on living independently, away from any neighbors. She was a slight woman with white hair, and she spoke in a gracious Georgian drawl. Her eyes sparkled as she embraced Wynton. It was her idea to have the band for dinner again. She and Wynton sat together at her dining room table. Soon they were deep in conversation.

She was talking about Texas. I asked if she knew that Louisiana people taught them what to do with a catfish. She started telling me about her life with her deceased husband, while the smell of Southern food wrapped around memories, heightening our expectation. She was talking about the old days and ways of ignorance that had happily passed. Spoke on the Civil Rights movement and what had changed and what had remained the same.

The range of people in the world stuns me. I may not remember the names of everyone I meet on the road, but I remember them. Not just how they looked but how they made me feel. Like the night in Monterey when Erik Telford came to the club, carrying his trumpet. The trumpet was bigger than him. He was too young to get into the club, but we could see his mop of blonde hair peeking up over the bottom of the window, bobbing and swinging. I gave him a lesson in the hallway, while the older customers were coming into the club.

Wynton also gave Erik his phone number and urged him to call. Erik did. A few years later, when the band came to the Monterey area again, Erik was there, and this time he got into the venue. Wynton would call Erik, too, to check if Erik had been practicing.

It was warm and fragrant in Monterey, though not as summerlike as it had been in Portland, a few days earlier. David Monette, who was still based in Chicago, had just flown in with a new horn. Wynton tried it backstage, before soundcheck, and then he switched back to the one he'd been playing before. Then he tried the new one again. While he was doing this a young woman stood off to one side of the room and stared at Wynton and listened. He looked at her and said, "Which of these horns sounds sweeter?" And then, before she answered, he also asked her name.

"Heather," she replied.

"Heather. Which of these horns sounds sweeter?"

"That one," said Heather, without hesitation pointing toward the new one.

"Heathers always know," Wynton said. "There it is."

Now, at the dinner in Georgia, Wynton was oblivious of time as he talked with Lee. But Lolis Elie began to worry about everyone's getting back to the theater for the first set. It was Lolis's fate to be concerned about such details; it was he, during his sojourn as road manager, whose assignment before early-morning hotel departures required him to wake everyone with the words "Bags at five" or "The bus leaves at six." Now, in this warm, convivial atmosphere so unlike the dressing rooms where the band often ate its post-sound-check, pre-concert meals, Lolis had to pry people from a third helping of catfish and cornbread or another glass of iced tea, firmly but with the diplomacy and tact not to offend Mrs. Anderson.

Soon Harold backed the bus out the dirt driveway of Mrs. Anderson's house, and on the drive back assured Lolis we wouldn't be late. "Piece of cake, ol' buddy," he announced.

By the time the bus reached the Georgia Theater the street had started to come to life, couples holding hands standing under trees as they watched the corner traffic before crossing. It was the kind of moment Wynton loved, even when he was not performing but just passing a theater.

By eight o'clock the theater was full. From the cramped dressing room behind the stage, where the musicians ironed and changed into their concert clothes, Wynton followed his band down a narrow flight of stairs that led directly to the floor of the stage. Applause began as soon as he stepped into the lights. After a brief "Good evening, thank you all for coming out tonight," he started right in playing, as if the long day had been merely an interruption in his music-making and now he was simply picking up from where he'd left off the night before, when the musicians had sustained an emotion with some counterpoint in a final blues.

In the second to last row a young woman with long brown hair and dazzling pendant earrings began to move her whole body within the groove of Wynton's "Jig's Jig," which opens with a seductively mesmerizing drum figure. As she sat, her shoulders pulsed. She seemed to be flirting with the man sitting to her right, someone else's date. The flirting stopped when Wynton began playing "Embraceable You." She listened to the music.

Until this song tonight, the people standing in the back of the theater had kept up a steady drone of conversation, but as Wynton continued playing the Gershwin the chitchat gradually ceased. Finally only one person was talking. A student in the row behind him whispered, loud enough for everyone to hear, "Shut the fuck up."

He did.

For an encore, Pine Cone played a tuba solo so powerful that the snares on one of Herlin's drums vibrated audibly. Reginald strutted out and did a kind of snake dance before joining in on Wycliffe's trombone. Three women in the front row stood up and danced in the space between the audience and the stage.

After the musicians got to the dressing room, Wynton continued playing while some of the men changed their clothes. As Wynton accented a tempo change, one of the band members paused, shook his hips, and started unbuttoning his shirt, slowly, pretending he was a stripper. The music became saucier. He put his tie between his legs and pulled it back and forth through his crotch. The others in the room started cheering.

It was late. In the audience, people heard the sound of a backstage trumpet, played now by Herlin and accompanied by a saxophone and trombone, and it triggered a holler. The holler started applause, faint at first, then louder and insistent. People in the aisles stopped and turned, facing the stage with its maze of microphones and music stands, wires, and instruments standing on holders. From their dressing room the men could hear the clapping.

"Let's go play a little more," Wynton said.

Herlin, wearing the slacks and sweatshirt he traveled in, grabbed the washboard by his drum set and followed Wynton across the stairs and into the audience. Wynton led the band up one of the two aisles, across the lobby, and then toward the other aisle. But by the time he reached the lobby, so many people had come back from the street into the theater that there was no clear opening to the other aisle. The volume level of cheering now competed with the second line music the band played.

Wynton could only move within a small space cleared by the people next to him. He inched toward the opened door and kept playing as, impulsively, he walked through it. He might march around the floor at clubs, or on a large outdoor stage, but never before from inside a theater out into the street. He held his trumpet at a high angle, the way a bugler would in a call. The parade continued under the marquee where he'd ridden the bicycle six hours ago. He knew the route from that ride and he followed it now, at a pace barely faster than a crawl, surrounded by hundreds of dancing, clapping people arranged in an irregularly shaped and continuously growing formation.

The night air was cool, but the rain predicted for the area had not yet started to fall. Passing Lee Anderson, Wynton stopped to play a musical thank-you for dinner.

Then, having come all the way around the block until the musicians reached their bus, still parked in the same space, Wynton paused again.

"Damn!" Wynton said to Harold and Darlene, who had

been napping during the second set. "This is what we do *for a living*!"

Tooting on a whistle and dancing, Rob marched near Wynton. Wycliffe feared he had been hitting people accidentally with his tuba. Women were kissing Wynton. Near the head of the parade was the woman with the long earrings.

At a bar across the street, the door had been propped open and the few people who had not come outside stood in the doorway and shouted to the throng. The band made a slow turn around the corner, and entered the theater again.

"Whew, that was a long block!" exclaimed Wess.

"Man, I was trying to find a shortcut through that parking lot," Wynton replied.

"That's something I always wanted to do," observed Wycliffe.

Finally the men were back in the dressing room, putting their instruments away.

"Close the door, it's drafty in here," demanded Herlin, in a mock stern voice.

Wynton remained in the theater signing autographs. Wess held his son Quad in his arms. Wess's wife, Desi, had flown in the day before from Baton Rouge, and the family had driven together to Athens instead of taking the bus. The way Wess held Quad, with such love and happiness, reminded me of the way he played his saxophone.

By the time Wynton had met everyone and signed everything and collected his clothes and horn, the gig had been over for more than an hour. An hour since their parade. Now the town was very quiet. But Wynton could hear Harold talking to Rob. They were standing behind the bus. A light rain had started to fall.

"What's wrong, Harold?" Rob asked.

"One of the batteries ain't working, pardner," reported Harold, dragging on another Marlboro.

It took Rob little time to process the information about the batteries. He understood clearly that the bus was not leaving Athens until the problem was fixed. He'd call a wrecker, he said.

"Can't be just any rig," explained Harold. "These batteries are lined up by their polarities and connected. They've got to be the right size or the bus won't never start."

Harold got back inside the bus while Rob asked Kyle Anderson to call a wrecker.

"Now, Harold, don't you be catching cold," said Miss Darlene, looking up from her Judith Krantz paperback.

Harold isn't going to catch a cold. There was a trip a while back when I was the first one up. Watching the road with Harold that morning, I was happy. There was a comfortable, empty seat by the bus door, but I sat on a storage compartment that also served as a stool, right next to Harold's upholstered chair. Me and Harold talking about roads and how America has changed and why he should stop smoking and country music and prejudiced rednecks and slutty groupies on rock tours and cops and pornography and the Civil War and the relative merits of the 410–gauge shotgun and fishing and whether there is a hell, and church people and the difficulties of marriage, political corruption, and why American coffee tastes like shit.

"Fuck, yes." Harold Russell said that morning, sliding the words off his tongue so "Fuck" had four or five syllables to it. "San Antone's less than an hour away." Filled with sleeping musicians, Harold's bus had cut a phantom-like figure across a Texas landscape. There was a chill in the air, before the high-noon heat, and sunlight brightened the mist from

a creek the bus had just passed. On the road, early that morning, Harold was pushing ninety—flying! *We talk about family. I tell him I hardly ever talk to my brothers. He had never been home for a son's or daughter's wedding. Harold and Darlene have six children and seven grandchildren, and they live all across the country, one married child in Idaho, another in Denver, another in Tucson, where Harold lived for ten years, around the time he was trucking. We agreed our track record was pretty pathetic. "We got to do better than this," we agreed. But deep down we knew we wouldn't.*

Now, in Athens, with the late hour and rain falling, the streets deserted and the cats in the band wanting to be back at the hotel, in their beds, Wynton heard Harold say the battery problem might take a while to fix. Wynton pretended to frown, shrugged his shoulders, and declared with certainty and gratitude, "Harold will fix it."

But even Harold could not fix the bus's dead battery. Nor could the first wrecker, nor the second; both had the wrong size charger. One by one, the men drifted off to their bunks, and most were asleep after three A.M. when the bus's diesel finally powered on. It would be five A.M. before the band was back in Atlanta.

When the bus pulled out, the orange parking cones had been removed. The bar across the street was closed. The bus's headlights reflected in the puddles that were already forming along the curbs. Only Miss Darlene remained awake up front, keeping Harold company as the band left Athens in the early-morning rain.

Why do they put the air conditioning vent right above my head, on the side wall of my bunk compartment?

I like the sound the bus makes when you are in your bunk, the gears changing when Harold goes up or down a hill or changes speeds. Even in a deep sleep, I always wake up when the bus pulls into a stop.

Wynton read Psalm 26 from the Bible. He knew it by heart. He even wrote a tune that the band recorded called "Psalm 26."

After he finished he reached over to the curtain side of his bunk where his trumpet case lay and unzipped one of the case's pockets. He began reading a chapter of a long essay by Thomas Mann. *I was a good student in high school, but we only had to read a few books a year. There is a lot I haven't read. Now I read all the time, novels sometimes and poetry, a lot of history and biography and essays. I like to read something challenging, something you can really attack and think about and relate to what is happening in music and in life. I never read mysteries or other escapism. I would; I mean, I have nothing against them. But I can't get interested.*

Time. It's been nonstop since I got out here. I'm always just coming off the road or going on. I've traveled all over the world, except for Africa, and I'm saving that for the right time. You got to be ready to go to Africa.

When the bus gears changed, Wynton knew when they had arrived in the hotel parking lot. The first one off the bus, he went straight to his room without speaking to anyone. He had slept a total of six hours in the last two days. But he was not going to sleep yet. Someone he knew was waiting for his call.

He used a special key to get the elevator to go to the top floor. The sky was beginning to lighten when Wynton walked into his suite. He put his trumpet case on one of the beds and picked up the phone.

Rob and a few of the others were going out. Wynton was not sure when they were leaving Atlanta; in fact he was not sure where they were going next.

Aren't we going to Alabama?

Wynton walked over to the window to watch the dawn. *When you see the sun rise in both Americas, throughout Europe, in the Far East, in Australia, you realize the sun is the same around the world. I have played my horn all over after the sun goes down. Done that since I was a boy and Branford and I would play gigs 'till all hours of the morning.*

It's all I know how to do.

One thing surprised me during the second line parade in Athens; about halfway around that block, we went right by some policemen, and they just looked in amazement. Whole hall full of people out in the street grooving. We must have been breaking some city ordinance or something. Eleven o'clock at night, all loud. They just stand there groovin'.

Lee Anderson and the dinner she gave us and the girl with the earrings. Veal and Homey. Cone n' Wes. The Deacon and Pete.

Second line.

The hotel where the band had been staying was toward the outskirts of Atlanta, in a flat area with quite a bit of open space around it. A Japanese company owned the hotel, which had the feeling of a building only a few years old. Everything in it was new and sleek, like in a health spa. You almost expected to see aerobic dancers working out in the lobby, except they'd have to be dressed up. Or not dressed at all, like the glitzy place near the hotel, a hi-tech strip club where the dancers didn't wear anything at all, spreading their legs for a ten-dollar tip. That was called a floor show. Though he had no problem with someone else going, Wynton would never be seen in such a club. Looking at women that way destroyed his sense of romance. Nor could he imagine having to pay someone to take her clothes off. *Paying takes all the fun out of it. The beauty in an encounter is the possibility of no.*

There was a waterfall in the hotel courtyard that you could see from the lounge in the lobby. That was where the dancers would have to be.

The day Wynton played before the Georgia State Senate, he had to walk through a rotunda to get to the senate chambers. The space around the stairs in the rotunda had been made into a kind of museum. There were flags on display, Confederate flags, including one that had flown at Appomattox.

Everything goes on in the world.

Wynton was warmly received. The senator who introduced him said he'd just been in Bermuda on vacation, and that Wynton's music was playing in the Bermuda airport. Many of the senators lined up afterwards to shake Wynton's hand. The lieutenant governor wanted someone to take a photograph of him and Wynton.

"That will help my image," he quipped.

Funny.

One of the senators said Wynton had just missed Bill Clinton.

"You got a bigger hand," he said.

Wynton looked out of his hotel window into the distant flatlands and hills all green. Where, he wondered, was the road that General Sherman had taken? Was it still there?

What a mean, hard tightass he must have been! Burning all those big plantations and houses, pitiless, just burning everything he and his men came upon and taking whatever they wanted. Whatever. Lord have mercy.

He wasn't bullshitting.

Wynton sat down again at the piano. In the music he was writing perhaps there would be something of Sherman. And the people whose homes Sherman had burned. And all those men who had fought that war, most of them poor white men who couldn't buy their way out of the draft, brainwashed into thinking the even poorer slave was what kept them down. They had to leave their women and children and then when they returned, if they returned, what they found was scorched earth.

And perhaps there would be dancers, ballerinas he knew, the dancers in the street by the Georgia Theater and some kids in West Oakland when he and Wycliffe played a love song. *When was that?*

Closing Time

It's four-ten A.M. Downtown at the Village Vanguard on Seventh Avenue, downstairs in the basement with its black walls and low black ceiling, the ghosts of Thelonious Monk and John Coltrane and Dexter Gordon mingle with the crowd that waited in the rain to get into the third set, which was supposed to begin at one o'clock but didn't start until nearly three. This is the last set of the septet's last gig and there is no reason to hurry. David Robinson is sitting at a table near the front of the stage, head bowed, eyes closed. "The end of a long road," he says. His sadness is palpable. A few minutes earlier the band played "Juba" from Wynton's epic *Blood on the Fields*, walking by each table after leaving the stage, and a man two tables from where Rob sits raised a black umbrella over his head and second-lined, moving the umbrella up and down in rhythm with the tune. Now the band is back on stage and the horns are playing the haunting, mellifluous long opening phrase of Duke's "Sweet & Pungent." Then three of the horns step back and quietly, slowly, Wynton begins his last blues of the night.

"Play it," Rob softly says from his table, not looking up, not opening his eyes. "Play those blues."

I'm sorry those people had to wait in the rain, but it feels good to know they want to hear the music. One hundred and fifty people waiting in the rain at three-thirty in the morning to hear some jazz music. I've been coming to the Vanguard for fifteen years. The first time I walked into this room I looked around at the pictures of all the cats and I said their names to myself. Monk. Trane. Hawk. Miles. It looks about the same, except it's Lorraine now in her red jacket tonight, not Max, who's in charge. She can be hard when you're coming in and someone with you hasn't bought a ticket.

"I don't care who they are, Wynton, they're staying right there in the hallway until I take care of my paying customers."

Later I saw her sitting with Mr. Murray and she started flirting. I can see her now at the back, by the door, listening to the music. Lorraine loves the music, that's why she's still here at this hour.

Lorraine.

"Play it," Rob says. "Play those blues, play those blues."

Kansas Blues

The ivory of the piano keys is cool like the breeze of a morning in the Louisiana spring. Outside, the rain pelting on the window makes puddles on the road, lit momentarily by the headlights of a truck passing through this lonesome town near the Colorado border. We are in Kansas again, a place called Hays in western Kansas. It is the middle of the night in the middle of the country. The loudest sound I have ever heard in my life, a single profound snap of thunder, has woken me from a deep sleep. So much space on the plains, the sound of the thunder has no beginning or ending. Just size. Wide awake, I lie in my bed and listen to the sound of smaller thunder before getting up and walking to the piano by the window. The bench feels hard and cold on my boodie. I am alone.

Two nights ago, we played a gig in downtown Kansas City, in an old burlesque house that had been fixed up into a theater for families to attend. I stayed late after the gig, visiting with people and giving a boy who had brought his horn backstage a trumpet lesson. The next morning we got in our bus and headed west to Hays, a college town so small that from the parking lot of our motel you could see the main commercial strip when you looked in one direction and nothing but Kansas cornfields when you turned around. It is dark in our space on the plains, dark and small, and all was calm until the thunder tore the blanket of silence that protected us.

Always moving. How many gigs in how many cities and towns. I always know when I am in America because there is a sense of struggle and energy, the energy of possibility, the energy of improvement and ascension. The struggle with the great uglinesses of our past. All the people we have degraded and lied to right here on these plains. How much unnecessary blood was spilled. In Alabama, Georgia, my beloved Louisiana. How much human potential destroyed because it came in a brown package. How many lies told and retold and how it diminished the quality of our national life. How much glory and heroism and saving of lives and celebration of freedom has sweetened our national history. Living in this tension makes me feel American and modern.

America is vast. I first realized that when I toured with Art Blakey in 1980. Every time we drove through New Jersey, on our way back to New York City, I would get excited about seeing the Manhattan skyline in the distance. I would think about where we had just played, about the Pennsylva-

nia hills and the jazz museum in Pittsburgh and Philly cheese steaks; or in New England, the way the tall, old trees look and the formality of the people. Just as I am thinking in Kansas about a gig a while ago in Montana, when some students got up at five-thirty to see us off. Five-thirty A.M. They were high school students, kids barely old enough to drive. Red. Erik Hanson. Went to Notre Dame and tried to get me to speak at his graduation and I couldn't go. I haven't heard from him in years. They think I've forgotten. But I'll always remember them and their car. The sun not yet up, morning cold, them just showing up to be with us, to find out who we were.

Montana. Kansas. I say the names as I did in school in Louisiana, learning geography. Nebraska. Arizona and New Mexico. Texas.

Texas is like a country in itself. Once I asked Rob to drive me to Amarillo from Houston. We thought it was a four- or five-hour ride. About two-thirty in the morning, after we had driven about five hours, we stopped at a gas station and asked, "Where's Amarillo?"

"Hell, son. You've got about seven hours to go."

And Rob's from Texas.

More thunder. The bells of heaven must be ringing. I switch from the ballet score I've been writing and play a few chord changes of Monk's "Ugly Beauty," the first two measures simply melody and bass moving to a chord, G seven, flat five. Monk. Just the name is enough.

I play my horn for a few minutes—with a Harmon mute, because I don't want to wake people up. That Harmon sound stings the air like a sip of whiskey after a mint. Not that I can imagine anyone sleeping through this Kansas thunderstorm. I sure wish somebody was here with me. We are supposed to be leaving for St. Louis soon. Four o'clock.

I call room service, but there is no answer. Most hotels have little refrigerators in the rooms with snacks and drinks that are marked up two hundred percent. You always swear you won't open it on principal, but I wish there was one in this room right now.

I put on some clothes and take the elevator down to the lobby, where there are vending machines. All is quiet. The lobby of the motel is built around an indoor pool, which has water in it that looks like formaldehyde. If you ever went on vacation with your family as a kid, this section of the motel is familiar. The lobby is humid and smells of chlorine, reminding me of the air in East New Orleans where refineries declared their presence on the wind. No one is in the pool at two A.M. No one in the lobby either. The billiard table where some of the cats were playing after we got back from the gig is empty, too. The last game frozen on the table.

The Coke machine takes my money, but when I press the button for a drink a red light comes on. When I press the coin return a red light comes on. I kick the machine. Always a stupid thing to do.

I limp down a hallway, past an empty dining room set for breakfast. The room has a strong odor of cigarette smoke. Really strong, like a club with heavy carpet and low ceilings. The front desk smells like that, too, but no one can be found. Ugly wallpaper with some old clocks on it. I continue outside. Our bus is parked by the entrance, but its engine is off. There will be food in the bus.

The air outside the hotel is cold and empty. Cleaned out by the storm. I picture the Kansas day that has just passed, with all the sleeping people in town, all the families and the people who live alone. Those who have no homes.

It is autumn. The corn is getting harvested. The hunters will follow; late fall is the height of the hunting season. I try to pic-

ture that as I stand outside the motel, smelling the autumn night air in Kansas. The crisp fresh air broken by the sharp snap of rounds tearing out the life of some unsuspecting animal, creating an instant carcass when the kill is clean. The Fourth of July firecracker smell of gunpowder eclipsed by bleeding, crying, and bleating when the kill is ugly. True. Something's got to die for you to live. Then you too. That's why we carry around one final prayer. Please Lord, let it be clean.

There was a mix-up this afternoon about transportation. Someone from the university thought I'd want my own car to take me to the workshop. I explained that we all went together. A television interview had been arranged in the lobby of the hall.

After the workshop we were taken to a dining room in a big empty building that reminded you of the way advertisements looked in the 1950s. Brown and green. The dining room was upstairs. Some tables had been joined together, and plastic chairs had been arranged around them. A gray, overlarge, high-ceilinged room that smelled of old paint. It created an incredible melancholy, as if people who ate here a long, long time ago were now dead. But this room remained, and the tables and chairs sat in frozen testimony to their existence. Anyway, there weren't enough chairs. And one of the caterers said, "We were told five people for dinner, not no nine."

"I'll eat at the motel," I had said, more than eager to leave. That was a big mistake.

During the Hays gig a lady sat on stage with us. She was someone we'd met coming into the hall. An older woman, in her sixties. She seemed so happy to be out. I asked her if she'd like to sit with us onstage. Most people would have said no indeed. She said yes. She sat there the whole gig, both sets, closest to the heat and intensity of that swing. When we were

*done playing and I introduced everyone in the band, I named
her, too, and she stood up and took a bow. Everybody in the
audience clapped for her too.*

Every night is different. Every night is a homecoming.

*A family came backstage after the gig. They had driven four
hours to get there. Their daughter played trumpet. I worked
with her breathing. They had to drive four hours to get home.*

*After I'd talked to everyone who came backstage, I returned
to my room, talking to people around the country on the
phone, kind of packing what had never really been unpacked,
looking through some papers, writing a little more new music,
looking at my too-big stomach and skinny legs, fat and skinny
at the same time. I just fell asleep there on the bed in my boxers. Boom!, the thunder.*

*With the door to the bus open, I hear the sound of some-
one's footsteps leaving the motel and disappearing into the
night. It is a woman's sound, heels, but I can't see her through
the tinted glass.*

*In the bus I finally get something to eat. Froot Loops, in a
plastic beer cup. There is milk, but no spoons, so I have to use
a fork.*

*It is still dark later, when we leave Hays. Nobody complains
about the hour—a little before five A.M. The lights along the
commercial strip of the town advertise old nasty greasy burgers
and diesel fuel. I get my Bible out of my bag and take it with
me to my bunk. Some of the cats are watching a flick on the
VCR in the back lounge. The Bible and a back-lounge movie
within two feet of each other.*

And the day comes alive.

III

at any moment

The band—now the Lincoln Center Jazz Orchestra—has just completed a tour that took it to Moscow, San Juan, and Rio de Janeiro. Burlington, Vermont, was the last stop on this tour. The band went up to Burlington from New York City and came back to the city the same day, passing right by Northampton, Massachusetts, on its way. The next day most of the musicians returned to Northampton by bus, with Wynton riding in a rented Jeep Wrangler driven by Frank Stewart. Nowadays when he's on tour, Wynton frequently rides in a van or a large Winnebago. He still avoids planes except when there is no choice. So, much of the time, he's still literally on the road.

But usually without Harold Russell at the wheel. With the larger ensemble that forms the Lincoln Center Jazz Orchestra, there is not enough room on Harold's bus for all the musicians. The bus they often take now is of a more standard interior design, with conventional seats, two abreast, and no kitchen or lounge. No bunks by the center aisle, no napping. Cone can't open the fridge and help himself to two servings of microwave chicken wings. The rear lounge, where in Harold's bus I once slept on a bed improvised between Homey's drums and someone's suitcase, is now a john.

By six o'clock on a Friday evening in early December a bus chartered for the day's runout from New York to Northampton is parked adjacent to the refurbished Calvin Theater, an old movie palace two blocks from the Iron Horse Café where I first met Wynton ten years ago. Because I live nearby, I can drive to Northampton; at odd hours, I have walked by the Iron Horse and stood outside, straining to remember the feeling of anticipation I experienced before my first Wyntonian gig so long ago. Now, seeing the bus by the Calvin, I know I'll find Wynton and the band inside, though I am afraid I have arrived too late for soundcheck.

And so I have. With my youngest child, Maren, holding my hand, I enter the theater through the backstage door and can hear only the sound of a trombone coming from the direction of the stage. It's Wycliffe fooling around, while Rob fusses with the placement of a microphone. Cone gives me and my daughter hugs; a few minutes later, seated at the piano, he starts scribbling a new tune on some sheet-music paper. He knows my daughter has been studying piano, and he asks her if she'd like to play something for him.

Shyly, she sits on the piano bench and begins a simple Bach minuet. Perhaps because she's a little nervous, she forgets a few measures at the end.

"Do you like to sing?" Wycliffe asks her.

Maren nods her head.

"Singing your songs will help you remember them when you play," Wycliffe says. "Here, let me show you."

Then, as my daughter beams in astonishment, Wycliffe plays her minuet, singing as he heard it.

"Now," Cone continues, "you try it."

While the two of them play the piano together in the empty theater, I stand off to the side of the stage and stare out and up, into the enormous balcony, where in just two hours a packed house will greet the band with a standing ovation. I remember the night in Boulder, Colorado, when Wynton was writing music for *In This House, On This Morning* at a piano in a second-floor hotel lobby. David Monette had come out on the road for that gig. Monette and I left him at the piano and went to dinner in a vegetarian restaurant, then walked the deserted streets, the wet night smelling of spring. At two A.M., Monette waved us goodbye. That was the night we climbed west, crossing the Rockies in Vail Pass. A few weeks later, in New Mexico's mountains and desert, Wynton would compose the $\frac{7}{4}$ clap and chorus of the work's climax. How many times afterwards did I hear the music—the night in Nice overlooking the sea and the night in Bayonne, when everyone in the audience picked up the $\frac{7}{4}$ beat and kept clapping afterwards, for the band, in $\frac{7}{4}$?

"We're not out here to be bullshitting," Wynton still likes to say, and he's still referring not only to the music but to the life.

"Dad." This is Maren, behind me, trying to catch my attention. Leaving my memories, I turn to her. "Cone says there's food downstairs."

Cone says. Here she is, ten years old, and she knows all the members of the band, many of them by nickname.

We find our way to the basement. On the stairway, coming up, we meet Wynton. Following him is a man I know, a local jazz DJ, who has been hoping to interview Wynton.

"We're going across the street to get some bread," Wynton says, as he catches Maren in his arms and squeezes her. I nod and smile. "Where are our 'hoes?" I want to ask, repeating in my head a phrase Wynton spent long hours teaching me to say as if it were one word, with poise and feeling and just the right inflection. *A phrase profound in its absurdity.* Coming out on the road again, over the years, I would pick up the house phone in whatever hotel Wynton was staying, ask for his room, and when he answered try to disguise my voice as I asked, "Where are our 'hoes?" He always knew it was me.

I do not say this now. In fact I do not really say anything. I try to be cool. Wynton asks Maren if she has been practicing, but there is no question of our coming with him since he is going to do his interview.

"Skain," I say, remembering the warm, sunny morning in Los Gatos on our way to Linda Oberman's café when I asked Wynton if I could use his nickname.

"Swig," he replies, smiling, and is gone.

thank you

To my wife Bonnie and our three children, Christian, Anna, and Maren; my mother, Ruth; my brother Nils, his wife Maddy, and their son Finn; and my sister Astrid.

To old friends and new, at home and on the road: Michelle Aldredge, Amherst College Music Library, Gabrielle Armand, Billy Banks and Lori, Joan Benham, Marsha Berkowitz, Janine Bertram, Jeff Blaustein, Rebecca Bolton, Susie Bonta, Gwen Briere, Cleve Bryant, Dr. George Butler, Gary Caron, Jehidith Cohen, the gang at Collective Copies, Happi Cramer, Deryle Daniels, Michelle D'Annunzio, Lesley Douglas, Steve Epstein, Susan Fromke, Nathan George, Peter Gelb, Mark Ghuneim, Rob Gibson, Kevin Gore, Bob Griffiths, Norton and Rikki Grubb, Hampshire College Library, Karen Hangsterfer, Kevin Hanover, Bill Hart, Jay Hassan, Hilary Hinzmann, Murray Horwitz, Sylvie Jacqueim, Andy Jaffe, Susan James, Dennis Jeter, Susan John, Laura Johnson, Edward Katzka, Emily Kimmel, Kent Laursen, Steven Lee, Steve Lembke, Janet Mac-

Fadyen, Donna MacLetchie, Bruce MacMillan, John Miller, everyone at the Monette shop (Dan, Dean, Gretchen, Dean, Tom), Kurt Masur, Peter Martins, Blanche Moyse, James Oliverio, Mark Pachucki, Steve Parkany, Miss Pearl, Lorraine Perry, Tom Piazza, Bob Polk, Annick Porter, Debby and Nancy at Preferred Travel, Susan Radin, Steve Rathe, Petra Ricterova, Harriet Rogers, John Schaffner, Stuart Schoffman, Denise Shannon, Shore Fire Media (Marilyn Laverty, Victoria Clark, Seth Cohen, Jim Flammia, Sara Haase), Jane Silverman, Norm Sims, April Smith, Jane Snyder, Laura Lee Spence, Lisa Stevens, Eric Suher, Grace Szwogolinski, John Tavenner, Christa Teter, Marty Townsend, Ralph and the guys at Validata, George Wein, William Whitworth, Bob Wilber, Mark Wilder, Larry Williamson, Bruce Wilcox, Andre Willis, Lisa Stewart Wrice, and the man in Charlotte, North Carolina, who brought food to my room after midnight though the hotel kitchen was closed, because, he said, "my mother told me no one should go to bed hungry."

To all the people in this book, especially Wynton and my brothers in the band, and to my offstage septet: Edward C. Arrendell II, Joe Bills, Wayne S. Kabak at William Morris, Andrea Schulz at Da Capo Press, Sheldon, Genevieve Stewart, and Kim Townsend.

—CV

Thanks to Ed Arrendell, Genevieve Stewart, Wess Anderson, Herlin Riley, Reginald Veal, Marcus Roberts, Todd Williams, Eric Reed, Ronnie Carbo, David Robinson, Eric Elie, Wycliffe Gordon, Carl Vigeland, Harold Russell, Miss Darlene, Delfeayo Marsalis, Herb Harris, Farid Barron, Victor Goines, Walter

Blanding Jr., Stephen Scott, Cyrus Chestnut, Ben Wolfe, Billy Banks, and Andrea Schulz.

—WM